NATURE ANATOMY
ACTIVITIES FOR KIDS
Fun, Hands-On Learning

KRISTINE BROWN, RH (AHG)

ILLUSTRATIONS BY KIM MALEK

ROCKRIDGE PRESS

Copyright © 2020 by Rockridge Press, Emeryville, California

No part of this publication may be reproduced, stored in a retrieval system, or transmitted in any form or by any means, electronic, mechanical, photocopying, recording, scanning, or otherwise, except as permitted under Sections 107 or 108 of the 1976 United States Copyright Act, without the prior written permission of the Publisher. Requests to the Publisher for permission should be addressed to the Permissions Department, Rockridge Press, 6005 Shellmound Street, Suite 175, Emeryville, CA 94608.

Limit of Liability/Disclaimer of Warranty: The Publisher and the author make no representations or warranties with respect to the accuracy or completeness of the contents of this work and specifically disclaim all warranties, including without limitation warranties of fitness for a particular purpose. No warranty may be created or extended by sales or promotional materials. The advice and strategies contained herein may not be suitable for every situation. This work is sold with the understanding that the Publisher is not engaged in rendering medical, legal, or other professional advice or services. If professional assistance is required, the services of a competent professional person should be sought. Neither the Publisher nor the author shall be liable for damages arising herefrom. The fact that an individual, organization, or website is referred to in this work as a citation and/or potential source of further information does not mean that the author or the Publisher endorses the information the individual, organization, or website may provide or recommendations they/it may make. Further, readers should be aware that websites listed in this work may have changed or disappeared between when this work was written and when it is read.

For general information on our other products and services or to obtain technical support, please contact our Customer Care Department within the United States at (866) 744-2665, or outside the United States at (510) 253-0500.

Rockridge Press publishes its books in a variety of electronic and print formats. Some content that appears in print may not be available in electronic books, and vice versa.

TRADEMARKS: Rockridge Press and the Rockridge Press logo are trademarks or registered trademarks of Callisto Media Inc. and/or its affiliates, in the United States and other countries, and may not be used without written permission. All other trademarks are the property of their respective owners. Rockridge Press is not associated with any product or vendor mentioned in this book.

Series Designers: Jane Archer and Karmen Lizzul
Interior and Cover Designer: Jane Archer
Art Producer: Sue Bischofberger
Editor: Laura Apperson
Production Manager: Jose Olivera
Production Editor: Melissa Edeburn

Author Photo by Andrew Dobson
Illustrations © 2020 Kim Malek

ISBN: Print 978-1-64739-834-7 | eBook 978-1-64739-531-5
R1

CONTENTS

Act Like an Explorer. Think Like a Scientist. iv

1 THE BIG BLUE SKY 1

2 THE GROUND BENEATH US 25

3 THE WATER THAT SURROUNDS US 47

4 THE PLANTS IN BETWEEN 63

5 THE CREATURES IN BETWEEN 81

Resources 95

Act Like an Explorer.
Think Like a Scientist.

Calling all young nature lovers! As you enjoy the great outdoors with this book, I want you to act like an explorer and think like a scientist. Why? Because both scientists and explorers use key observational skills in their work to establish accurate and reliable information for the rest of the world. Scientists and explorers follow five basic steps whenever they conduct an experiment, study nature, or come up with new ways to do things.

The first step is to **observe**. Scientists and explorers observe the situation or object they are studying. For example, American agricultural scientist George Washington Carver (1860–1943) observed that some cotton crops were not thriving. He noticed that crops that were rotated with peanuts and sweet potatoes grew much better. The peanuts and sweet potatoes improved the soil for the cotton, resulting in larger cotton harvests.

The second step is to **ask** many questions. Galileo di Vincenzo Bonaulti de Galilei (1564–1642) was an Italian astronomer, physicist, and engineer who studied the night sky. His many questions about the night sky led him to create a version of the telescope that let him view the stars up close. With his new telescope, he was able to better observe the night sky and answer his own questions.

The third step is to **imagine**. Scientists and explorers use their imagination to answer their questions, which arise from their observations of their environment. English botanist and photographer Anna Atkins (1799–1871) used her imagination to figure out how to make images of seaweed. Her imagination led her to place specimens directly onto paper coated with chemicals that turn the paper blue when exposed to the sun, thereby creating a silhouette effect. Using the process, she published a series of cyanotype books.

The fourth step is to **test**. Percy Lavon Julian (1899–1975) was an American chemist who observed that plants contained medicinal properties. He asked many questions, which led him to imagine that scientists could create synthetic (or human-made) versions of the medicinal properties of plants. He decided to test his theory by creating synthetic versions of the plants he studied.

The fifth step is to **reflect** on the work that's been done. English naturalist, geologist, and biologist Charles Robert Darwin (1809–1882) observed many plant and animal species and asked many questions, which led him to conclude that species arise and change over time through natural selection. Before publicizing his theory of evolution, which contradicted the prevailing view of creation, he had to reflect on everything he had studied and tested to make sure he was correct.

As you complete the lessons and activities in this book, you will follow in the footsteps of explorers and scientists by observing, asking, imagining, testing, and reflecting. My hope is that you will become a lifelong steward of Earth and continue to apply these five skills throughout your life.

HOW TO USE THIS BOOK

You will find this book easy to navigate. There are five chapters, each of which contains a theme related to our natural world: the sky, the earth, water, plants, and animals. Each chapter contains several lessons that are paired with an activity to get you thinking about nature as you observe, ask questions, imagine outcomes, test ideas, and reflect on your findings. Everything in this book is designed to help you better understand the natural world around you. Feel free to skip around and do the lessons and activities that you find most interesting or those that correspond with the time of year. Let's take a closer look at how each chapter is set up.

THE LESSON

This book contains 20 lessons divided into five chapters. Each lesson focuses on a basic element of nature and gives you an objective, or goal. For example, in chapter 1, the goal of The Phases of the Moon lesson on page 16 is to understand why the moon changes appearance throughout the month.

Each lesson teaches you to think like a scientist and act like an explorer with thought-provoking questions to inspire you to explore the topic.

ACT LIKE AN EXPLORER. THINK LIKE A SCIENTIST.

After reading each lesson, you'll test and prove your ideas by using your observation skills. Later, you'll reflect by journaling your thoughts about the experience.

THE ACTIVITY

An activity accompanies each of the 20 lessons. Step-by-step instructions help you apply scientific principles from each lesson just as a scientist would perform an experiment. These instructions are preceded by a list of materials you'll need and prep work you'll need to complete beforehand.

Some activities require you to be cautious or to ask an adult for help. These activities include a Safety First warning. You'll also find tips on how to adapt an experiment, if necessary, and to troubleshoot any issues that might arise.

THE NATURE JOURNAL ENTRY

In addition to this activity book, you'll need a journal to keep track of your experiments and write your answers to questions. You'll describe what you see and what you're doing, and you'll note any questions that come up and how you tested ideas. Your journal is also the place to reflect on the activities and their outcomes and answer the journal prompts that are listed at the end of each section. You may also want to sketch pictures as visual reminders of each activity.

You can use any type of journal you'd like. If you think you'll be doing a lot of drawings, you may prefer a blank journal. If you think you'll be doing more writing than drawing, choose a lined journal. You can also choose a dot grid journal, which gives you guidelines for writing but still provides plenty of blank space for drawing if you think you'll be doing a lot of both. Some of my favorite journals are listed in the Resources section on page 95.

Setting up your nature journal is easy! Once you have chosen a style of journal, write your name on the first inside page (there's often a space for this) and the date you start the journal. Once your journal's filled, you can write the date you complete it on the same page.

To begin using your nature journal, you may choose to start a new section for each activity. Make a heading with the lesson and activity you're working on, and

ACT LIKE AN EXPLORER. THINK LIKE A SCIENTIST.

add the date you begin that lesson. Then write down any questions you have, as well as answers to the questions in the activities and journaling exercises.

You may also choose to divide the book into 20 sections by taking the number of pages (many journals are numbered) and dividing it by 20. An adult can help you with this step! For example, if your journal has 140 pages, dividing 140 by 20 gives you seven pages for each activity. Every seven pages, write the name of the activity in sequential order (the order they are listed in the book), then dedicate those seven pages to that activity.

From there, you can either fill in the pages as you do each activity or you can further divide the pages to create categories for each activity. For example, you can include headings such as "Observations," "Questions," "Imagined Outcome," "Testing the Idea," "Journal Prompts," and "Sketches." Choose the way that you like best.

Now that you've got an idea of how this book works, dive in and start exploring!

ACT LIKE AN EXPLORER. THINK LIKE A SCIENTIST.

THE BIG BLUE SKY

This chapter invites you to look up! What do you see in the sky? The sun? The moon? Stars? Clouds? A storm? Lightning? What about the things you don't think you see, such as the atmosphere? Or things you hear, such as thunder? What about the things you may not necessarily see in the air but are all around you, such as the changing of the seasons?

In this chapter, we'll go over many aspects of that big blue space above us and answer many common questions about the natural elements of the sky.

LESSON

Exosphere
400–40,000 Miles

Thermosphere
50–400 Miles

Mesosphere
31–50 Miles

Stratosphere
11–30 Miles

OZONE

Troposphere
Up to 10 Miles

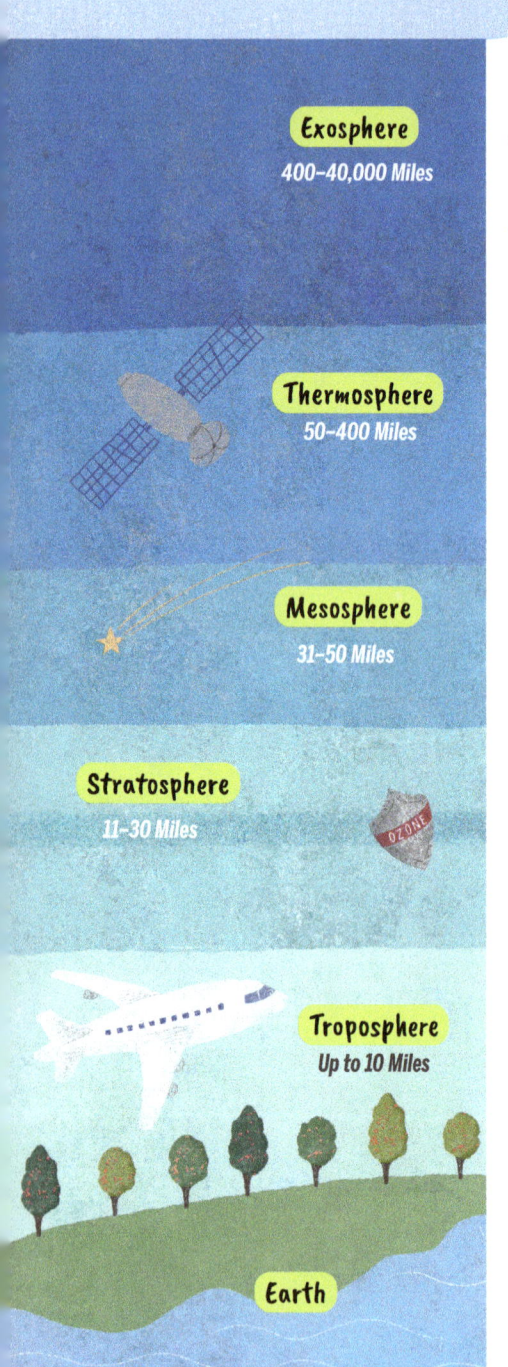

Earth

LAYERS OF THE ATMOSPHERE

We call the sky, which is layers of various gases, the atmosphere. The atmosphere protects us from radiation from the sun and other sources, keeps our temperature from becoming too extreme, gives us the air we breathe, and recirculates water back to Earth.

The atmosphere is made up of five layers of gases, including the troposphere, stratosphere, mesosphere, thermosphere, and exosphere. The air is very dense close to Earth but thins out farther away from Earth. Let's take a look at these layers a bit more closely.

Troposphere. Closest to Earth and extending 10 miles into the sky, the troposphere circulates our water through evaporation and transpiration, condensing the water into clouds that get heavy then release the water, in the form of rain, back to Earth. The troposphere also contains three-fourths of the mass of the entire atmosphere. This layer is where commercial airplanes fly.

Stratosphere. Extending 20 miles from the troposphere is the stratosphere, where the ozone layer is found. The ozone layer is the protective layer of the atmosphere that shields us from harmful ultraviolet radiation emitted by the sun.

Mesosphere. The middle layer is the mesosphere, reaching 31 to 50 miles above Earth.

The mesosphere is the coldest layer, and space debris generally burns up when it hits this layer.

Thermosphere. The fourth layer, the thermosphere, is broken into the ionosphere and the magnetosphere and extends 50 to 400 miles out from our planet. This layer is where satellites orbit Earth. The beautiful and colorful northern lights are created in the magnetosphere layer from magnetically charged particles, and the ionosphere allows long-distance radio wave communication.

Exosphere. The final, extremely thin layer of our atmosphere is the exosphere, found 400 to 40,000 miles out from Earth.

Fun Fact

DO YOU KNOW WHY THE SKY IS BLUE?

Most sunlight, which contains all the colors of the rainbow, shines through our atmosphere. Blue light, however, has a shorter wavelength than other colors of light. The blue light is absorbed by gases and particles in the atmosphere, giving the appearance of a blue sky.

Exosphere
400–40,000 Miles

Thermosphere
50–400 Miles

Mesosphere
31–50 Miles

Stratosphere
11–30 Miles

Troposphere
10 Miles

Earth

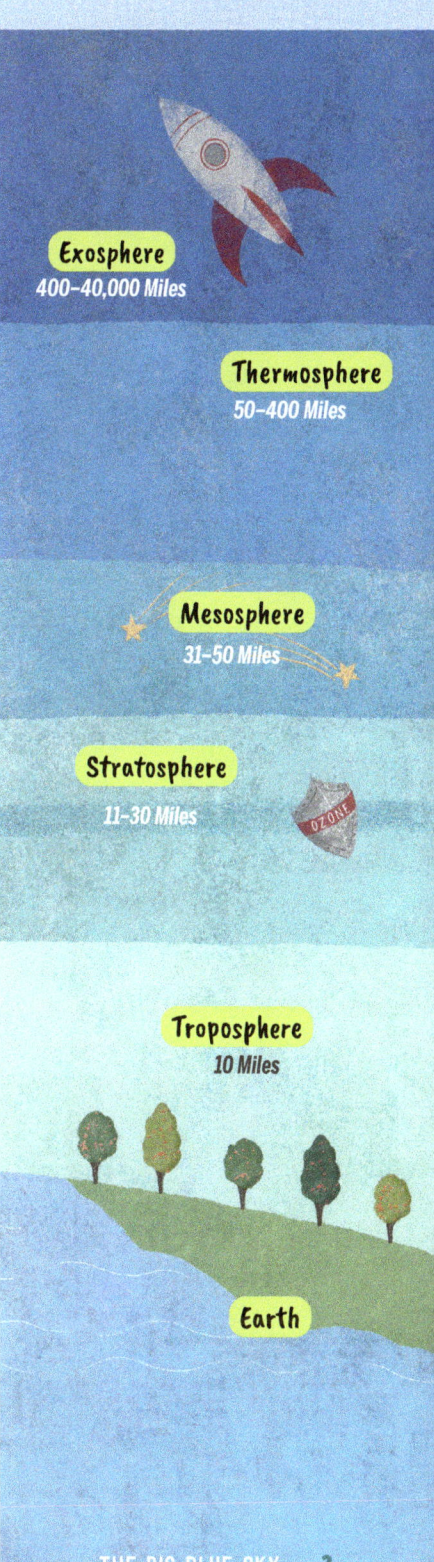

THE BIG BLUE SKY

ACTIVITY

WEIGHING AIR

TIME:
15 TO 20 MINUTES

CATEGORY:
INDOOR, EXPERIMENT

MATERIALS
PIECES OF STRING, ABOUT 12 INCHES EACH (4)

BALLOONS, ALL THE SAME SIZE AND NOT FILLED WITH AIR (4)

MASKING OR PAINTER'S TAPE

DOWEL ROD OR YARDSTICK

We can't see the air that surrounds us, so does that mean it has no weight? How do you even weigh air to find out? In this experiment, you'll determine whether air—even though you can't see it—has weight.

PREP WORK

1. Loosely tie each piece of string to a balloon.

2. Use the masking tape to secure two of the strings (with the balloons attached) to one end of the dowel rod. Tie the remaining two strings to the other end of the rod.

3. Balance the rod horizontally on your finger.

4. Make a mark over your finger where the rod is evenly balanced with two balloons on either side.

INSTRUCTIONS

1. Look at the rod as it balances on your finger. Notice how the balloons on either side pull down to help the rod remain balanced. Why do you think it's currently balanced?

2. Make an illustration in your journal of how the rod and balloons look now.

3. What do you think will happen if the balloons on one side of the rod are filled with air? Can you imagine what that would look like? Write down what you imagine will happen and draw a quick sketch in your journal of how you think it will look if two of the balloons on one side are filled with air.

TIP

➡ If you have trouble trying to balance the rod on your finger, cut a fifth piece of string to tie to the center of the rod. Now, you can balance the rod by holding the string.

4. Set the rod down and carefully untie two of the balloons from one side.

5. Blow up both of the balloons and tie them off so the air stays in them. Carefully tie them back onto the rod.

6. Balance the rod back on your finger. What happens? Does the rod stay balanced? If not, which side tilts up and which side tilts down? Why do you think that happened? Sketch in your journal how the rod looks now.

7. Can you get the rod to rebalance by moving the filled balloons closer to the middle or farther away from the middle? Why do you think this helps to rebalance the rod?

CONCLUSION:

In this lesson, you learned that the troposphere was the densest layer in the atmosphere, holding three-quarters of the mass in the entire atmosphere. Even though we can't see air, it does have weight! We can move the filled balloons closer to the center to help redistribute the weight and bring balance back to the rod.

NATURE JOURNAL ENTRY

Now that you've learned about the layers of the atmosphere and seen a demonstration that proves air has weight, answer these questions to reflect on what you've learned.

1. *Why do you think air has weight?*

2. *What do you think would happen if you added air to one of the empty balloons on the other side of the rod?*

THE BIG BLUE SKY

LESSON

WEATHER, SEASONS, AND STORMS

Did you know that where you're located geographically determines the type of weather and seasons you'll experience? What does the climate look like where you live? What does it feel like? If you live near a beach, you may experience lots of warmth and sunshine. Sometimes hurricanes may appear in the ocean near you, causing lots of wind and rain. If you live up in the mountains, winters are probably colder and filled with lots of snow. If you live in the plains, summer lightning storms and tornadoes are often a possibility for your area.

We describe weather as a natural event that brings about sunshine and rain, clouds and lightning, thunderstorms, tornadoes, hurricanes, and more. Weather can be broken into four seasons: spring, summer, fall, and winter. Depending on where you live, the seasons mark changes in weather, temperature, and the amount of daylight. Two equinoxes and two solstices mark the amount of daylight every year. Some places experience four distinct seasons, whereas others have similar weather for two seasons or more. Let's take a closer look.

Spring. This is the time of year that you'll see equal amounts of day and night if you live away from the equator (people living near the equator see equal days and nights year-round). The *spring equinox* marks the time in spring when both day and night are equal in length. After the spring equinox, days gradually lengthen while nights shorten. During the spring, Earth starts to warm up and plants start to emerge from the ground after disappearing over the winter. Cold winter temperatures give way to milder spring temperatures.

Summer. During the summer, days are longer and nights are shorter. The longest day of the year is called the *summer solstice*. After the summer solstice, each day starts to gradually shorten while the night gradually lengthens. During summer, plants are lush, flowering, and often start fruiting. This time of the year can be hot, humid, and muggy, depending on where you live.

Fall. Also referred to as autumn, fall is another time of year that provides equal amounts of day and night, but during this time of year, the days start to shorten and the nights begin to lengthen. The *fall equinox* marks the time when both day and night are equal in length. Nights get longer from here. In fall, leaves begin falling from deciduous trees and plants begin dying back. Temperatures start to drop as the season heads into winter.

Winter. Nights are longest and days shortest in winter. The longest night of the year is called the *winter solstice*. After the winter solstice, the nights get shorter again. In winter, most plants have died back, and in colder locations, snow often falls instead of rain. The temperature turns cold, requiring many animals (such as bears, snakes, and bats) to hibernate, so they can avoid the cold and lack of food.

Clouds are closely related to weather. They are formed when water evaporates from Earth. The water vapor clings to dust particles in the air and forms into clouds. If the clouds accumulate too much water, they become too heavy and form rain.

Ten different cloud types can be found anywhere from 1.24 to 3.73 miles into the atmosphere. (That distance is equivalent to 4.5 to 13.5 Empire State Buildings stacked end to end!) Recall that this part of the atmosphere is called the troposphere (see page 2). The troposphere has three layers. The *lower layer* is about 1.24 miles away from Earth, the *middle layer* is about 2.49 miles away, and the *top layer* starts about 3.73 miles away. Different types of clouds form in these layers. Let's take a closer look.

Stratus. These clouds form in the lower layer. They appear on overcast days and hang low. They are gray, flat, and typically fill the entire sky.

Nimbostratus. These clouds form in the lower layer. They are dark gray but may appear a bit fluffy. When you see these clouds on the horizon, you know rain is coming soon.

Stratocumulus. These clouds form in the lower layer. They can be gray or white, or a combination of the two, and are fluffy in appearance. They appear in patches.

Cumulus. These clouds form in the lower layer. They are the big, white, fluffy clouds that you watch on a warm summer day as you lie back on the ground and gaze up at the sky. Though their tops are white, the bottoms are gray.

LESSON

Cumulonimbus. These clouds form in the lower layer. However, they are found in all three layers, starting at the lowest layer and developing vertically into what we call an "anvil head" that ranges all the way up to the top layer. These clouds indicate rain and can bring about severe weather, including heavy rainfall, hail, and tornadoes.

Altocumulus. These clouds form in the middle layer. Smaller than stratocumulus clouds, altocumulus clouds are small puffy clouds that are white to gray and are the most commonly seen clouds in the sky. These clouds are most often seen in the summer and can indicate that storms are on their way or that a cold front is moving in.

Types of CLOUDS

- 6 miles — Cirrostratus
- 5 miles — Cirrocumulus, Cirrus
- 4 miles — Altocumulus, Altostratus, Cumulonimbus
- 2.5 miles — Stratocumulus, Cumulus
- 1.2 miles — Stratus, Nimbostratus

Altostratus. These clouds form in the middle layer. They are gray and hang in sheets across the sky, allowing the sun to dimly shine through them. They generally indicate a warm front is on the way, though if they are combined with cumulus clouds, they can indicate a cold front instead.

Cirrocumulus. These small, white clouds, made of ice crystals, form in the top layer. They are less commonly seen and generally appear in the winter or when it's cold outside. Some people call them cloudlets because they are so small.

Cirrostratus. These transparent, whitish clouds form in the top layer and cover the entire sky. When they are present, you will see a halo around the sun or moon. These clouds generally indicate a warm front is moving in.

Cirrus. These clouds form in the top layer. These wispy clouds streak across the sky, curling upward on one end. They are white and, like cirrocumulus clouds, are made up of ice crystals instead of water.

Fun Fact

DID YOU KNOW THAT THE SEASONS ARE REVERSED IN THE SOUTHERN AND NORTHERN HEMISPHERES?

When it is summer in the Northern Hemisphere, it is winter in the Southern. Spring and fall are also reversed.

ACTIVITY

MAKE A CLOUD

TIME:
15 MINUTES

CATEGORY:
EXPERIMENT, INDOOR

MATERIALS
⅓ CUP HOT WATER

JAR WITH A LID, SUCH AS A CLEAN EMPTY PICKLE JAR

ICE CUBES

SMALL CAN OF AEROSOL HAIR SPRAY

Have you ever wondered how a cloud is formed? Have you ever gone into the mountains, hoping to touch a cloud, only to find that the clouds disappear when you are among them? This activity will help you see how clouds are formed from a combination of water and warm and cool air, which creates vapor.

Safety First: *Use caution with the hot water, so you don't burn yourself.*

PREP WORK

1. Gather your items together, so they are ready to go.

INSTRUCTIONS

1. Pour the hot water into the jar, and swirl it around to warm up the glass.

2. Place the lid upside down on the jar, so it forms a small tray. Fill the lid with ice cubes.

3. Let the ice sit in the lid for 20 to 30 seconds.

4. Set the can of hair spray right next to the jar. Position the nozzle where the lid meets the top of the jar. Quickly lift the lid a little, spray a good squirt of hair spray into the jar, then set the lid back down, leaving the ice on top.

TIP

→ *If you're having trouble getting the hair spray into the jar quickly, have a parent, sibling, or friend help you with this step.*

NATURE ANATOMY ACTIVITIES FOR KIDS

5. Watch the jar and see what happens. Based on your observations, can you guess what is creating the cloud? What is the hair spray mimicking? What will happen if you open the lid?

6. Lift the lid and watch the cloud disappear into the air.

NATURE JOURNAL ENTRY

This lesson covered a lot! From the seasons, equinoxes, and solstices to the 10 different types of clouds that fill the sky, you learned many things that happen in the troposphere. Reflect on everything you learned, and answer the following questions in your journal.

1. *Why do you think the cloud formed when the hair spray was introduced into the jar? Do you think the "cloud" was there before you added the hair spray?*

2. *Have you ever seen fog rise from the ground? What do you think creates the fog? Do you think fog is the same thing as a cloud? What makes it different from a cloud?*

CONCLUSION:

In this lesson, you learned that clouds are formed from evaporated water that rises from Earth into the sky. This activity demonstrates this action as warm water and air turn to vapor in the jar and rise to meet the cold air near the lid, which pushes back down on the water vapor. When the hair spray is sprayed into the jar, it mimics dust particles in the air, giving the vapor something to cling to and forming a cloud.

THE BIG BLUE SKY

LESSON

SUNRISE AND SUNSET

Have you ever woken up early in the morning to see the sunrise? Or watched the sunset? What brings about the reds, oranges, purples, and yellows? In the Layers of the Atmosphere lesson (see page 2), you learned why the sky is blue. The colors of sunrises and sunsets are on the opposite end of the color spectrum from blue.

When the sun rises and sets, it "sits" at a longer angle away from Earth. As the short blue light waves bounce, they get deflected away from our eyes, becoming too small to see. The longer red and yellow light waves can still reach our eyes, causing the beautiful range of colors in the morning and evening.

The sun rises in the east every morning and sets in the west every evening. Although the sun seems to move from east to west throughout the day, it is

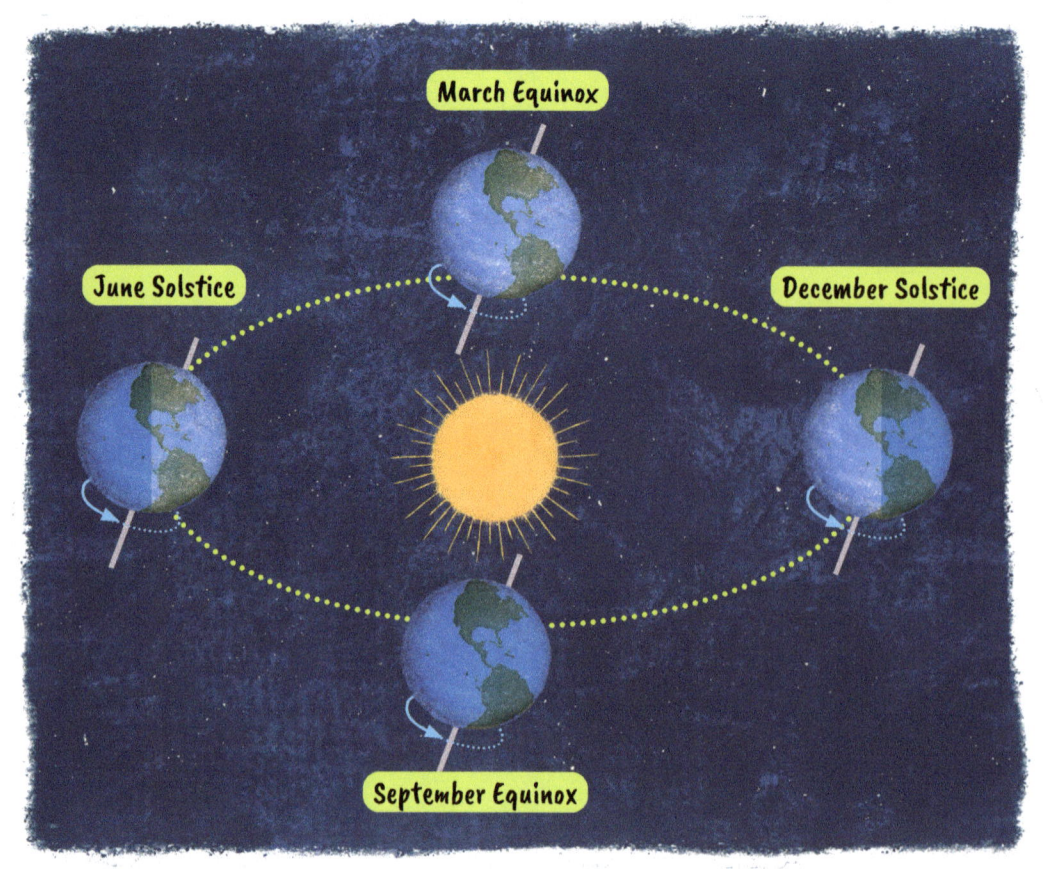

LESSON

actually stationary. Rather, Earth rotates, or orbits, around the sun, all while rotating toward the east. It takes Earth 24 hours to complete one full rotation, which is why one day is 24 hours.

Before clocks, people told time by the sun. When the sun is directly overhead, it is roughly noon. When you know when the sun rises and sets, the horizons can be broken up between the rise/set time and when the sun is directly overhead. You can then split that space evenly into the hours between rise/set and noon, and the time can be counted off. Adults can hold their hands below the sun in the evening and gauge how long until sunset by counting the number of fingers from the horizon—four fingers represent one hour. Since your hands are smaller, each hand will count for about 30 minutes.

In addition to Earth orbiting around the sun—which takes one full year—and spinning on a rotation, Earth also tilts closer and farther away from the sun, which creates our longer and shorter days. The June and December solstices mark the longest or shortest day of the year, depending on your hemisphere, and the March and September equinoxes mark dates in which day and night are exactly the same length.

That's a lot of movement! We'll talk more about all this movement in the next chapter.

Fun Fact

DID YOU KNOW THAT WHEN THE EARTH TILTS CLOSER TO THE SUN, IT'S WINTER? AND WHEN EARTH TILTS FARTHER AWAY FROM THE SUN, IT'S SUMMER?

You'd think that being closer to the sun would make us warmer. However, as Earth's orbit nears the sun, we get less daylight and our days shorten, and as it moves away from the sun, we get more sunlight and our days lengthen.

THE BIG BLUE SKY

ACTIVITY

TELLING TIME WITH THE SUN

TIME:
30 MINUTES TO MAKE THE SUNDIAL, PLUS A FEW MINUTES TO OBSERVE

CATEGORY:
CRAFTS, OBSERVATION, OUTDOOR

MATERIALS
WHITE PAINT
PAINT BRUSH
PLYWOOD BOARD, ABOUT 12 × 12 INCHES
RULER
PENCIL
NAIL, 6 INCHES OR LONGER
HAMMER

TIP

→ If you don't have a piece of plywood and large nail, you can use a piece of cardboard painted white and a pencil or dowel rod. The sundial won't be as permanent, but it will last quite a while.

Have you ever used a sundial to tell time? As the sun travels across the sky, its shadows mark time throughout the day. Many ancient civilizations, including the Mayans in Central America, used sundials to keep track of the hours of the day. The accuracy of a simple sundial depends greatly on your latitude, so keep that in mind!

Safety First: *Be careful when hammering the nail.*

PREP WORK

1. Use the white paint and paint brush to paint your board on one side, then let the paint dry.

2. Using the ruler, diagonally line up two corners and lightly draw a line with the pencil in the center of the board.

3. Repeat this step with the other two diagonal corners to create an "X" in the center of the board.

4. Use the hammer to carefully tap the nail into the center of the board, just deep enough so it won't fall out. Now you have a sundial!

INSTRUCTIONS

1. Begin setting up your sundial early on a sunny day. Observe your yard for a day to find an ideal spot. Set your sundial on level ground in full sun, in a location where it will not be disturbed.

2. Once you set your sundial down, mark where the sun's shadow falls at the top of an hour, such as at

6 a.m. Use the ruler to draw a line from the nail to the edge of the board and label it with the time.

3. Draw a line along the shadow and mark the hour every hour until sunset. Can you guess where each hour's shadow will land before sunset? After watching the pattern emerge, sketch the sundial in your journal and mark where you think the shadows will land. When you've finished marking the true sundial, go back to your journal and compare your results to your guesses.

4. Use your sundial to tell time.

NATURE JOURNAL ENTRY

Now that you've seen how time can be tracked as Earth rotates, turning us toward and away from the sun, reflect on all you've learned. Answer these questions in your journal.

1. *Can you think of other ways ancient people used the sun to mark time?*

2. *How important do you think the marking of time was to ancient people?*

3. *Why do you think many cultures built stone circles, such as Stonehenge, which mark the solstices and equinoxes?*

CONCLUSION:

Even though your regional location may need some adjusting for the time to be completely accurate, it's easy to see how ancient people harnessed the sun to keep track of their days. In this lesson, you learned about sunrises and sunsets. You learned that their colors are created by the angle of the sun, which happens when Earth rotates, making the sun appear to rise and set. This also helps us mark time, as you learned with this sundial activity.

THE BIG BLUE SKY 15

LESSON

THE PHASES OF THE MOON

The moon is a fascinating sphere that orbits around Earth, taking 27.3 days to make a complete orbit. Unlike Earth, the moon does not spin as it orbits, which means we always see the same view of the moon's surface from here on Earth. Although the moon can look very bright, it does not give off its own light. Instead, the moon's surface reflects the light of the sun, which makes it appear to glow. Although the moon is much smaller than the sun, it appears to be the same size as the sun because it is much closer to us than the sun is.

The moon orbits Earth counterclockwise, but because the moon does not rotate, the sun always hits the same side of the moon. However, we can't always see the lit side of the moon here on Earth, which makes it look like the moon's shape is changing. During a complete orbit around Earth, the moon can be seen in eight different phases. Let's take a closer look at them.

16 NATURE ANATOMY ACTIVITIES FOR KIDS

New moon. The beginning moon phase is known as a new moon. During this time, the moon isn't visible because it is between the sun and Earth. A solar eclipse can only happen during a new moon.

Waxing crescent moon. As the moon orbits around Earth, the sun catches it at an angle, giving us a waxing crescent moon. Because of the position of the sun and moon, this sliver looks like a backward "C."

First quarter moon. About seven days into the moon's cycle, the first quarter moon appears. During this phase, the moon is side by side with Earth, and we see its illuminated right half.

Waxing gibbous moon. When the moon is three-quarters full, it is known as a waxing gibbous moon.

Full moon. Fourteen and a half days into its cycle, the moon becomes a full moon as Earth is fully between the sun and moon. A lunar eclipse can occur only during a full moon.

Waning gibbous moon. As the moon continues to orbit Earth, the bottom fourth vanishes. This phase is known as the waning gibbous moon.

Last quarter moon. When the moon is side by side with Earth again (this time on the opposite side), it is again half lit by the sun. We call this phase the last quarter moon.

Waning crescent moon. The final phase of the moon is the waning crescent, and, again, only a sliver of the moon is illuminated—this time, in the shape of a normal letter "C."

Fun Fact

DID YOU KNOW THAT PEOPLE ONCE THOUGHT THE MOON HAD SEAS ON ITS SURFACE?

So they named the dark spots we see *lunar maria*, which means "moon seas" in Latin. Later, these dark spots were discovered to be remnants from volcanic eruptions that happened within the past three billion years (with some as recent as 10 million years ago)!

ACTIVITY

THE MOON CYCLE

TIME:
A FEW MINUTES EVERY NIGHT FOR 30 DAYS

CATEGORY:
OBSERVATION, OUTDOOR

MATERIALS
PENCIL

QUARTER

YELLOW AND GRAY MARKERS, COLORED PENCILS, OR CRAYONS (OPTIONAL)

Have you ever gazed up at the moon and wondered what phase it was in? Or why it keeps getting bigger and smaller each month? Just how long does it take the moon to complete a cycle? In this activity, you will observe and chart the shape of the moon every night for an entire cycle.

PREP WORK

1. In your journal, use the pencil to trace the quarter 30 times over the course of the page. This will help you keep track of the moon phases. You may want to create two columns of 15 circles each or three columns of 10 circles each. Make sure to leave enough room to the right of each circle to make a note of the phase.

INSTRUCTIONS

1. Beginning at any time during the moon's cycle, observe the moon at night. Use the pencil or markers (if using) to fill in the first circle in your journal with the shape of the moon. Next to the shape, write down the date (month and day), time, and the phase of the moon.

2. After your first night of observing the moon, do you think the moon will continue to increase or decrease in size? Where do you think the sun is located in conjunction with Earth and the moon?

3. Continue filling in the circles each night, starting at the top of the first column and working your way down, then continuing with the next column, until all 30 circles are filled.

TIP

→ Try starting this activity with the new moon, so you can see the progression of the moon every night.

NATURE ANATOMY ACTIVITIES FOR KIDS

4. Keep trying to estimate how the moon will continue to change, and record any thoughts you have on your observations, as well as how correct you were.

TIP

→ If a night is cloudy and you can't see the moon, leave the circle blank and make a note of it. The next night, after you've filled in the moon's shape, compare that shape with the shape from two nights ago. Fill in the missing night with a shape between the two.

NATURE JOURNAL ENTRY

This lesson taught you all about the phases of the moon. Reflect on this lesson and activity as you answer the following questions in your journal.

1. *Did the moon appear at the same time every night?*

2. *Was the moon the same size every night? If not, why do you think the size also changed?*

3. *What was your favorite phase of the moon and why?*

CONCLUSION:

This activity helped you prove that as Earth orbits around the sun and the moon orbits around Earth, the moon appears to change shape every day. Over the course of a month, the moon waxes (or more of it becomes visible) until it is a complete circle. After the full moon, the moon wanes (or less of it becomes visible) until it is completely gone from the night sky. The pattern on your paper should mimic the sun's reflection on the moon.

THE BIG BLUE SKY

LESSON

LOOK UP AT THE STARS

Take a walk outside during a new moon—away from the light pollution of the city if you live in one—and you'll see billions of tiny lights dancing across the sky: stars!

Stars, like our sun, are made up of gases (hydrogen and helium) that form a hot ball with a core of nuclear fusion. Some stars live to be trillions of years old, until they burn up all their hydrogen fuel.

Ancient people did not know this about stars but held them in high regard. Navigators used stars to help them travel at night, staying on course by using the North Star as their guide. People connected the dots of star groupings, called constellations, and imagined them to be various creatures such as Cetus, the sea monster, or mythological people and creatures such as Orion.

Because people did not have televisions, cell phones, or even books to entertain themselves, stories were a popular past time. Ancient cultures and civilizations created stories about groups of stars—stories passed along through generations. Today, the International Astronomical Union recognizes 88 constellations, 12 of which are the signs of the zodiac, most of which reflect names and lore from Greek mythology.

Because of Earth's rotation and orbit, we see different constellations at different times of the year. For instance, in the Northern Hemisphere, Orion can be seen only in the fall and winter.

Can you think of any stories about constellations? Have you ever looked up at the sky and noticed the stars forming a shape? What story emerged from that image?

Fun Fact

DID YOU KNOW THAT PEOPLE IN THE NORTHERN HEMISPHERE SEE DIFFERENT CONSTELLATIONS THAN PEOPLE IN THE SOUTHERN HEMISPHERE SEE?

These constellations remain constant, never rising or setting, and they are referred to as circumpolar constellations.

ACTIVITY

CREATE A CONSTELLATION

TIME:
30 TO 60 MINUTES

CATEGORY:
CREATIVE WRITING, INDOOR/OUTDOOR, OBSERVATION

MATERIALS
HEADLAMP OR FLASHLIGHT

PENCIL

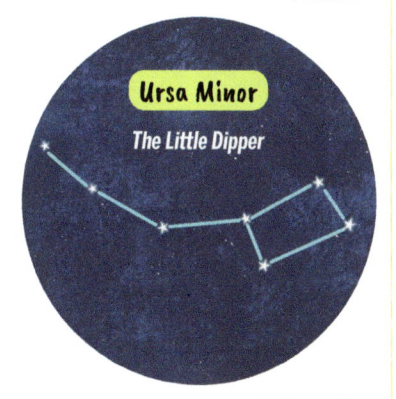

Ursa Minor
The Little Dipper

TIP

→ You may wish to use a stargazing app to help you locate and chart your patterns, but don't let the app dictate the patterns you see. Create a constellation that fits your world view.

Do you ever look up at night and watch the stars? Do you know any of the constellations in the sky? Have you ever wondered how they were created or who created them? Have you ever made up your own constellations by observing patterns of stars? In this activity, you'll look at the stars in the sky, find a pattern, and sketch it, then make up a name for your new constellation and a story to go with it.

PREP WORK

1. Go outside on a clear night, preferably when the moon is new, so the moon's light won't block your sight.

2. Look up at the stars and observe any patterns you see appearing. Don't try to find existing constellations that you know. Instead, use your imagination to see if new patterns emerge. With the billions of stars in the sky, you'll start to see patterns easily.

3. Imagine how ancient civilizations must have viewed the sky. Ask yourself what they might have seen and what they might have thought about all the stars they saw in the sky.

INSTRUCTIONS

1. After observing the sky for a while, does a particular pattern keep jumping out at you? Can you use your imagination to create a shape from the pattern you see?

2. Turn on the headlamp and use the pencil to sketch the pattern in your journal, noting any particularly large stars in the pattern.

THE BIG BLUE SKY   21

ACTIVITY

3. Note the location of your pattern in the sky—is it in the south? West? North? East? Use any landmarks to help you remember the location, such as "right above the oak tree in our backyard" or "to the right of the building next door."

4. Go inside and connect your star dots to create your shape if you haven't already. Create a name for your constellation—perhaps it reminds you of your dog? Or maybe your favorite action figure or superhero?

5. Write a story that explains the name of your constellation.

NATURE JOURNAL ENTRY

In this lesson, you learned how the constellations came to be created by ancient people from all cultures around the world. Reflect on the lesson and activity as you answer these questions in your journal.

1. *Why do you think stargazing was so popular in ancient civilizations?*

2. *What are some of your favorite existing constellations and why?*

3. *How do the constellations in the Southern Hemisphere differ from the ones in the Northern Hemisphere?*

CONCLUSION:

This activity helped you experience how the constellations were created. Ancient people all around the world saw patterns in the stars and named them as reminders of the events, people, animals, or myths in their everyday lives. Though these are official constellations now, we shouldn't stop observing and adjusting these ideas to fit our modern world. The constellations that we know today were named hundreds of years ago (or longer) to share ideas and events of the time.

- Hematite
- Clay
- Mica
- Halite
- Magnetite
- Chalcophyrite

THE GROUND BENEATH US

On chapter 1, we explored the atmosphere and beyond. Now, let's come down to Earth and investigate what our great planet is made of and how it ticks.

We'll start by exploring the difference between rotation and revolution and how they affect our sunlight and weather. Then we'll go deeper into the core of Earth to find out what it's made of. Next, we'll explore the crust, or top layer of Earth, and all the rocks and minerals found there. Some of these really old rocks form fossils, and we'll study how they are made and what they can tell us about the past. Finally, we'll explore the different types of landscapes that make up our beautiful Earth and break them down into different types of landforms.

LESSON

HOW THE WORLD SPINS

Earth is always spinning—or rotating—around its own axis in a counterclockwise motion. The axis is an invisible line that goes through the center of Earth, through the north and south poles. If you were to observe the spin of Earth, you would notice that Earth's axis is not straight up and down but tilted, which is known as the axial tilt.

Billions of years ago, Earth did spin around on an axis that was straight up and down; however, another planet collided with Earth and left a dent in it. That planet fell into orbit around Earth and became our moon. The old axis line is called the obliquity line and it runs perpendicular to the orbital, or equator line. See the illustration on page 27.

As you learned in chapter 1, Earth takes 24 hours to complete one rotation on its axis. One rotation equals one day. We can't feel Earth move because it is such a large object compared with us, but in reality, it is rotating at almost 67,000 miles per hour! That's about 120 times faster than the average commercial jet flies.

In addition to rotating around on its own axis, Earth also revolves around the sun. Some people refer to the Earth's movement around the sun as a *rotation*, but it is actually a *revolution*, which means "to go around an object." It takes Earth 365.25 days to make one complete revolution around the sun. The location of Earth in its revolution around the sun creates our equinoxes and solstices (see page 6).

Fun Fact

DID YOU EVER WONDER WHERE LEAP YEAR COMES FROM?

Because it takes one-quarter of a day to complete our annual revolution around the sun, every four years we use the equivalent of an entire extra day to revolve around the sun. To account for it, we add that day—February 29—to our calendar once every four years and call it a "leap year."

ACTIVITY

THE DIFFERENCE BETWEEN NIGHT AND DAY

TIME:
15 TO 20 MINUTES

CATEGORY:
EXPERIMENT, INDOOR, OBSERVATION

MATERIALS
GLOBE
DARKENED ROOM
FLASHLIGHT

Diagram labels: Obliquity, 23.4°, N, Equator, Orbital, Ecliptic Plane Around Sun, Earth's Axis, Perpendicular to the Ecliptic, S

Have you ever wondered how night and day happens? Or why we experience day while people living on the other side of Earth experience night? Or why there are different time zones all around the world? In this activity, you'll create a model of Earth spinning to understand how night and day are created and why only half of Earth experiences day at one time.

PREP WORK

1. Set the globe on a table or other flat surface, so you can easily spin it with one hand while holding the flashlight with the other.

2. Close the blinds or curtains, and turn off any lights to darken the room, so you can better observe where the light falls.

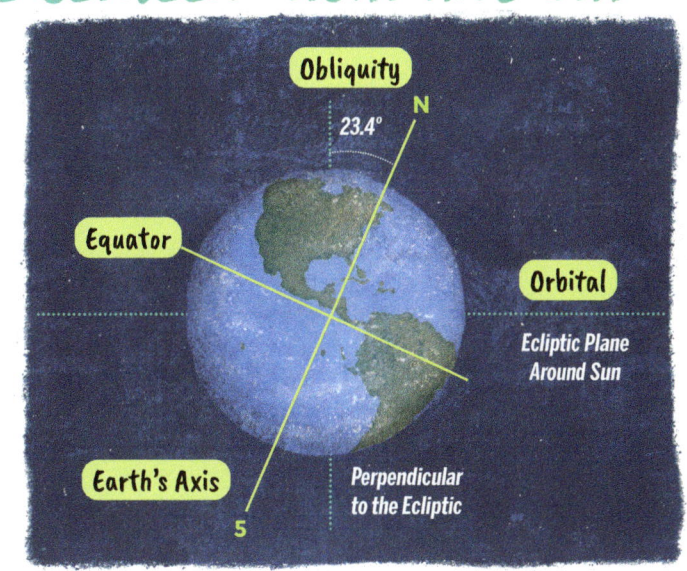

TIP

→ You might find it helpful to have someone hold the flashlight and spin the globe for you, so you can more fully observe the day and night reflections from the flashlight on the globe.

THE GROUND BENEATH US   27

ACTIVITY

INSTRUCTIONS

1. Think about Earth's rotation and observe the globe. Why does the sun first appear in the east and set in the west? What do you think will happen when you shine the flashlight on the globe?

2. Imagine the flashlight as the sun, shining onto Earth from one side. Turn on the flashlight, and hold it off to the side, pointing it at the center of Earth. At the same time, start spinning Earth in a counterclockwise direction.

3. What's happening with the light from the flashlight? Is the entire globe lighting up or only a portion of it? Though you are spinning your globe much faster than the actual Earth appears to spin, remember that one entire spin equals one day.

CONCLUSION:

You just proved that the sun can only shine on one side of Earth at a time. As Earth spins on its axis, the sun lights half of Earth, creating day, while the other half of Earth faces away from the sun, creating night. People created different time zones, so the sun appears to rise and set at about the same time no matter where you are on Earth. This way, everyone has a regularly scheduled day and night.

NATURE JOURNAL ENTRY

Now that you've learned about Earth's rotation on its axis and how day and night are created, as well as the seasons and the length of a year, reflect on what you've learned. Answer these questions in your journal.

1. *Describe what happened in this activity and add a sketch to show how the sun lights only part of Earth at a time.*

2. *In the morning, which part of your country does the sun appear in first?*

3. *What would happen if we didn't add an extra day to our calendar every four years?*

28 NATURE ANATOMY ACTIVITIES FOR KIDS

LESSON

EARTH'S LAYERS

On Earth's surface, we can easily observe soil, but is the entire planet made of soil—all the way to its center? Actually, soil is only part of one of Earth's four main layers, which include the inner core, outer core, mantle, and crust. Let's take a closer look at Earth's layers, starting at the center of our planet and working outward.

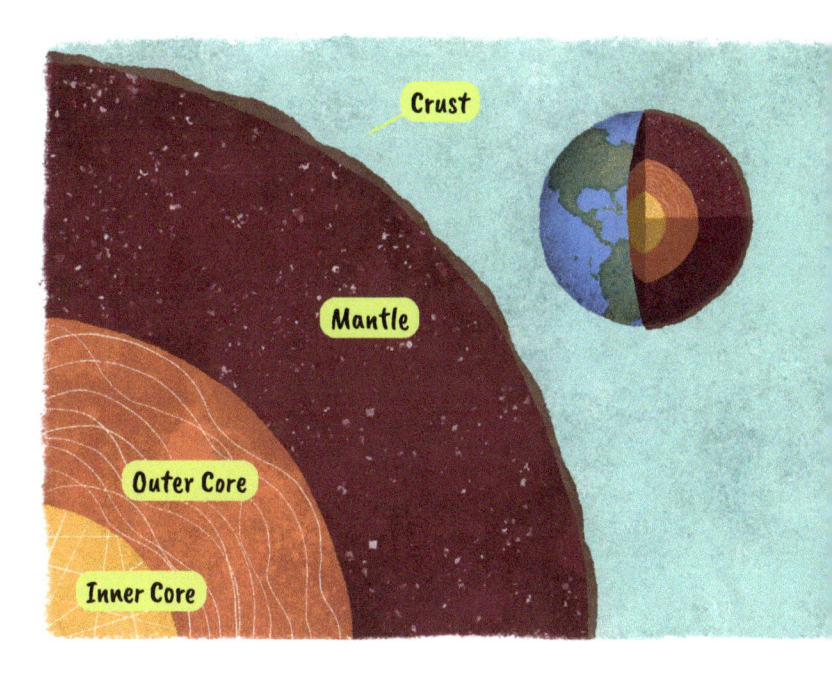

Inner core. The inner core, located in the very center of the earth, is a solid sphere made up of iron, nickel, gold, silver, platinum, palladium, and tungsten. The core is 1,500 miles across, which is roughly the size of half of the United States. Because of the pressure on the inner core, it remains solid even though its temperature can be 10,000 degrees Fahrenheit (more than 10 times hotter than lava) or higher.

Outer core. The outer core is about as thick as the inner core it wraps around. The outer core layer is liquid iron, reaching a temperature of 10,345 degrees Fahrenheit. Being liquid, the outer core spins much faster than Earth spins, which creates Earth's magnetic field.

Mantle. The mantle is split into two parts, the upper and lower. The lower mantle is closest to the outer core and is mostly solid and less dense than the upper mantle. The lower mantle ranges in thickness from 400 to 1,800 miles, and can be up to 7,000 degrees Fahrenheit. The upper mantle is 200 to 250 miles thick, is semi-molten to solid, and has a temperature range of

THE GROUND BENEATH US 29

LESSON

900 to 1,600 degrees Fahrenheit. The upper mantle contains more iron and magnesium and less silicon than the crust.

Crust. The crust is the thin outer layer of Earth. It ranges from 3.1 to 43.5 miles thick and is mostly made up of silica and aluminum. There are two different types of crust: the continental crust and the oceanic crust. The oceanic crust is found where the oceans are and includes dense rocks made of igneous materials from volcanoes and magnesium. The continental crust creates our continents and is thicker, made from rocks that are full of aluminum, oxygen, and silicon. The oceanic crust covers 60 percent of Earth, and the continental crust covers 40 percent.

The crust and the upper mantle are made up of different pieces, which we call tectonic plates. These plates fit together like puzzle pieces but are all slowly moving at different speeds and in different directions—away from one another, past one another, and sometimes into one another. When they collide, the plates can become locked together, creating what we call a fault line.

Eventually, they build up so much energy from moving that a shock, or seismic, wave occurs. In the ocean, a seismic wave creates a tsunami, a giant tidal wave that can crash onto a continent and cause a lot of destruction. If a seismic wave happens on a continent instead of in the ocean, an earthquake occurs. Movement from the tectonic plates can also cause explosions, volcanos, and landslides.

Tectonic movements are responsible for the formation of mountains, the expansion of the seafloor, and the regulation of temperature.

Fun Fact

DID YOU KNOW THAT THOUSANDS OF EARTHQUAKES OCCUR AROUND THE WORLD EVERY DAY?

Though most of them are so small that only special machines can detect them, these shifts in our tectonic plates are continually reshaping the continents and oceans.

NATURE ANATOMY ACTIVITIES FOR KIDS

ACTIVITY

CREATE A 3D EARTH MODEL

TIME:
30 TO 60 MINUTES

CATEGORY:
CRAFTS, INDOOR

MATERIALS
PIECE OF WAX OR PARCHMENT PAPER

WORK SURFACE

SIX DIFFERENT COLORS OF CLAY: RED, ORANGE, YELLOW, BROWN, BLUE, AND GREEN

ROLLING PIN

BUTTER KNIFE

Scientists observe the layers of Earth using seismic waves. From these observations, scientists have been able to create a model of Earth's layers. You can use your skills of observation to recreate a three-dimensional model of Earth using clay and the information from the lesson.

Safety First: *Be careful when using the knife to cut into your model Earth.*

PREP WORK

1. Gather your supplies and lay the wax paper on top of your work surface.

INSTRUCTIONS

1. Look at the diagram of the layers of Earth on page 29. You will create your model from this illustration.

2. Ask yourself which layers appear to be the thickest and which appear to be the thinnest.

3. Using the orange clay, roll out a ball about 1 inch in diameter. This ball will represent the inner core.

4. Using the rolling pin, roll out the red clay until it's about ½ inch thick. Carefully wrap this layer around the inner core, smoothing it out until the inner core is completely covered. This layer represents the molten layer of the outer core.

5. Next, roll out the yellow clay to a ¼- to ½-inch thickness. This layer represents the lower mantle, which varies in thickness. Wrap this layer over the outer core

TIP

➡ If you want to hang your model, screw a small eye hook into the top before drying it (for self-hardening clay) or baking it. After your model is dried, you may want to paint it with a clear sealant, such as Mod Podge, to make it shiny.

THE GROUND BENEATH US

ACTIVITY

and carefully smooth it in place, being careful not to squish the emerging Earth you are creating.

6. Roll out the brown clay until it's about ¼ inch thick. This layer represents the upper mantle. Apply it as you did the lower mantle.

7. You are almost finished! Roll out a thin layer of blue, just enough to cover the entire upper mantle. Once you've applied this layer to your Earth, roll out some green pieces, and use your imagination to create the continents on Earth.

8. Once you've created your Earth, it's time to cut into it, so you can see all the layers! Carefully use the butter knife to slice from top to bottom, halfway into Earth.

9. To reveal Earth's layers, repeat this cut a few inches to the right to cut about one-quarter of your Earth.

CONCLUSION:

You demonstrated that Earth is made up of four layers. These layers can be solid or liquid depending on the temperature and presence of pressure. Scientists learned about these layers using seismic waves to record the types of materials each area of Earth contained. By using this information, you were able recreate your own model of the layers of Earth.

NATURE JOURNAL ENTRY

You just learned all about the layers of Earth and the seismic activity in Earth's crust and upper mantle. Now it's time to reflect on what you've learned. Answer these questions in your journal.

1. *Why do you think it's impossible to dig through all the layers of Earth?*

2. *Although explorers have been able to map out most of the continents by physically exploring the continental crust, the greatest depths of the oceanic crust have not been so easy to explore. How do you think scientists are helping explorers to learn about the shape of the oceanic crust?*

Igneous   Sedimentary   Metamorphic

ROCKS AND MINERALS

Earth's crust contains many types of rocks and minerals. Rocks and minerals are *inorganic*, which means they don't come from plants or animals. They are also *natural objects*, which means they come from Earth and are not man-made.

Do you know the names of some of these rocks and minerals? Take a moment to think of all the ones you can name and write them down in your journal.

Minerals are made of the same chemicals and have the same structure the whole way through. Minerals can be found in all kinds of materials, including inside of our own bodies. One familiar example of a mineral is salt. There are four different classes of minerals: carbonates, oxides, silicates, and sulfides. Let's take a closer look.

Carbonates. Carbonates make up a small percentage of Earth's crust and are composed of a combination of calcium and carbon, called calcite. Carbonates are found in all three types of rocks.

Oxides. Oxides make up a small percentage of Earth's crust and are created with oxygen and another chemical element. Oxygen and iron combine to make magnetite, which can be found in 3 percent of Earth's crust.

Silicates. Silicates make up the largest percentage of Earth's crust and contain a combination of silicon with other chemical elements. The two most common types of silicate minerals are quartz, which contains silicon and oxygen and makes up 12 percent of the crust, and feldspar, which contains minerals such as aluminum, calcium, sodium, and silicon, and makes up about 51 percent of Earth's crust.

LESSON

Sulfides. Usually metallic in appearance, sulfides make up a small percentage of Earth's crust and contain many valuable minerals such as silver, zinc, lead, copper, and iron.

Minerals and rocks are similar and can be hard to tell apart. The main difference is that rocks are made from two or more minerals clumped together. Rocks can be all kinds of textures, from hard to soft. Three types of rocks that are found in Earth's crust: igneous, metamorphic, and sedimentary. Let's take a closer look.

Igneous. Igneous rocks are created when the magma from an erupted volcano solidifies. When the magma cools, rocks and minerals form. Most igneous rocks contain silicate minerals and some sulfide minerals. Granite is an example of a common igneous rock.

Metamorphic. Extreme conditions, including high temperatures and lots of pressure over time, can transform igneous and sedimentary rocks into metamorphic rocks. Some common metamorphic rocks are marble, quartzite, and slate.

Sedimentary. When igneous rocks are weathered over time by water, pressure, wind, and heat, their chemical composition changes, and sedimentary rocks form. As igneous rocks are weathered down into smaller particles, they are carried away by water sources, such as glaciers and rivers, or by the wind until they settle and build up. As these small particles of rock become compacted, they harden and become sedimentary rock over long periods. Common sedimentary rocks include limestone, coal, and sandstone.

> **Fun Fact**
>
> DID YOU KNOW THAT ROCKS AND MINERALS ARE PART OF YOUR EVERYDAY LIFE?
>
> You will most likely use more than three million pounds of rocks and minerals in your lifetime!

Both rocks and minerals have been mined for use in everything from building materials, pavers, watches, computers, and cell phones to dietary supplements, sandpaper, paint, and matches. Can you think of any materials in your home that are made from rocks and minerals?

ACTIVITY

Making Paint from Rocks and Clay

TIME:
1 TO 2 HOURS

CATEGORY:
CRAFTS, INDOOR/OUTDOOR

MATERIALS
SOFT ROCKS IN A VARIETY OF COLORS (AS MANY AS YOU'D LIKE)

OLD PILLOWCASE

HAMMER

SAFETY GOGGLES

SOIL AND CLAY IN DIFFERENT COLORS (AS MANY AS YOU'D LIKE)

STONE MORTAR AND PESTLE

SMALL METAL MESH STRAINER

JARS OR OTHER CONTAINERS (ENOUGH TO MIX PIGMENTS AND STORE DRIED PIGMENTS)

POWDERED GUM ARABIC

WARM WATER

Many of our paints today, including water and oil paints, are made with natural pigments from the earth. You can create your own palette of natural pigment paints from the rocks and soil that are all around you. If you have access to a natural stream, you will most likely find clay and soft rocks along its banks. You can use both to make paint.

Safety First: *Be careful when smashing rocks with a hammer as the fragments tend to fly all around. Wear safety glasses and have an adult help.*

PREP WORK

1. You will need to conduct two tests with your rocks to make sure they are suited for making into paints. The first test is to use your rocks to draw on the sidewalk or on another larger rock. If your rock leaves a mark, it will likely make a great paint.

2. Next, you want to test out your rocks to make sure they are soft enough to use. Place them one at a time in the pillowcase, and using your hammer and wearing your safety goggles, carefully give them a good whack. If they break, they are good for making pigments. If they do not break, they are most likely too hard to grind down.

3. If you've collected soil or clay, it most likely has water in it. Set it outside in the sun to dry out.

4. Sort your rocks and soils by color. If you have more than one of the same color, keep those together.

THE GROUND BENEATH US

ACTIVITY

Ask yourself what colors you think they'll make. Imagine what each paint color could be used for.

5. Wearing your safety goggles, place a rock in the stone mortar, and use the pestle to start grinding your rocks into a fine powder. The finer the powder, the smoother your pigments will be. If you have more than one rock of the same color, only grind one at a time.

6. Place the mesh strainer over one of the jars and pour your powder into the strainer. Shake the powder through the strainer and return the larger particles to the mortar and pestle.

7. Continue to grind the larger particles into a powder, then strain it into the jar.

8. Repeat this process until you have ground down all the rocks, soil, and clay that you'd like. Be sure to pour each new color into a new jar.

9. Label each jar with the rock, soil, or clay you used. In your journal, make a list of the materials you used, where you found them, and the color they produced. To keep an even better record, you may find it helpful to add drawings or photographs of your materials.

INSTRUCTIONS

1. To make paint, you will need a bit of your pigment and a binder, something you add to the pigment to help it stick together. It will also help your paint stick to the surface of the thing you're painting. Many ingredients, including egg whites, honey, and oil or animal fat can make great binders. For this activity, you will use gum Arabic, which is made from the sap of a tree.

> **TIPS**
>
> ➡ You might want to leave one rock intact to place in each jar to help you better identify each color.
>
> ➡ Paint a dab of color onto the jar label of your paint and your powdered pigment, so you will know which color each pigment makes when used.

2. Place ¼ teaspoon of gum Arabic into a clean jar. Add ¾ teaspoon of warm water to the powder and stir to dissolve.

3. Add ¼ teaspoon of your chosen pigment to the jar and stir to combine. You may need to add more pigment; play around with the texture until it's thick enough.

4. Paint a swatch of the color in your journal, making a note of the type of binder you used.

5. Repeat this step with any other pigments you want to use, all in separate jars. Your paints are ready to use! What will you paint with them?

6. Store your paints in sealed jars.

CONCLUSION:

Many rocks and minerals exist on Earth, and many of them are used in your everyday life, often in ways you don't realize. In this activity, you learned that paint is one of these uses. By grinding down rocks into a powder, you were able to create pigments that could be added to a binder to make paint.

NATURE JOURNAL ENTRY

You've gotten a glimpse at how much we incorporate rocks and minerals into our everyday lives. Now it's time to reflect on what you've learned. Answer these questions in your journal.

1. *What are some items in your home that you didn't realize were made from minerals?*

2. *What are some items you did realize were made from minerals?*

3. *When you made your paint pigments, were there any colors that surprised you once you made your paints? If so, why?*

THE GROUND BENEATH US

LESSON

FOSSILS

Do you know what a fossil is and why they are so important? Have you ever found a fossil when exploring outdoors? Fossils are the remnants of plants and animals from long ago that became trapped in the earth. When these remnants are trapped under layers of sediment, fossils are made. Over long periods, the sediments harden and create an imprint of the plant or animal that was there. After millions of years, as sediments settle and shift, these fossils may become exposed.

Often explorers, called archeologists, dig them up when they explore a location. Fossils are similar to the nature journal you are keeping—they are records, documenting life that lived millions of years before we did. Fossils can tell us many things, including the age of the stone in which the plant or animal was trapped, the evolution of a species, and the climate that existed when the plant or animal lived.

Fun Fact

DID YOU KNOW THAT ONLY THE HARD TISSUE OF PLANTS AND ANIMALS CAN BECOME FOSSILIZED?

The soft parts rot away long before the process takes place.

38 NATURE ANATOMY ACTIVITIES FOR KIDS

ACTIVITY

MAKE YOUR OWN FOSSIL

TIME:
1 TO 2 HOURS

CATEGORY:
CRAFTS, INDOOR

MATERIALS
SILICONE CUPCAKE LINERS AND PLASTIC WRAP OR ALUMINUM FOIL

PLAY-DOH OR OTHER SOFT MODELING CLAY

VARIETY OF NATURAL OBJECTS (AS MANY AS YOU'D LIKE)

PLASTER OF PARIS

PLASTIC CONTAINER, SUCH AS AN OLD YOGURT CONTAINER

SPOON

TIPS

➡ Use the spoon to smooth the plaster of Paris you poured into the molds. Your fossils will sit on a surface once removed.

➡ You can also press plastic versions of insects or other creatures into the Play-Doh to create your fossils.

A real fossil cannot be made in a single afternoon, but you can make a replica of a fossil to get an idea of how they are formed and to see what they look like. In part one of this activity, you'll make a simple mold, and in part two, you'll use it to create a fossil. You'll want to gather a variety of objects to create your fossils. Some things that would make great fossils include pinecones, acorns, shells, leaves, flowers such as echinacea or daisies, bones, nutshells, seeds, and sticks.

Safety First: *Have an adult help you mix the plaster of Paris and be careful not to breathe in the powder.*

PREP WORK

1. If you're using silicone cupcake liners, line each cup with plastic wrap. If you're using aluminum foil, tear off a square for each object you're fossilizing and form the square into a circular dish. These will be your fossil containers.

2. Line the bottom of the prepared containers with a piece of Play-Doh that's about ½ inch thick.

INSTRUCTIONS

1. Observe your natural objects. Where did each one come from? List the objects you are using and where they came from in your journal. Imagine what kind of fossils your objects will make.

THE GROUND BENEATH US 39

ACTIVITY

2. Press one object into the Play-Doh in each container, making sure the most textured side of the object is pressed into the Play-Doh.

3. Carefully remove all the objects, and set the containers aside.

4. Mindfully mix the plaster of Paris in the plastic container according to the instructions on the package.

5. Using the spoon, transfer the plaster of Paris into each container, being sure to get into all the cracks and crevices of the Play-Doh molds without damaging the impressions.

6. Let the plaster sit until it is completely dried, about 1 hour. While the plaster's drying, make a sketch of each object you are fossilizing.

7. Once the plaster is dried, carefully pull away the containers and Play-Doh from the plaster of Paris. You should have detailed fossils of your objects!

CONCLUSION:
Millions of years ago, plants and animals became fossilized when they died and their remains were buried by sediment. Their soft tissue rotted away, but their hard tissue didn't and was replaced by minerals in the sediment over time. In this activity, plaster of Paris mimicked sediment in a sped-up version of fossilization, helping you get a glimpse of how fossils are made.

NATURE JOURNAL ENTRY

Fossils teach scientists about the history of the world. You just made your own fossils that you can study just like a scientist. Now it's time to reflect on what you've learned. Answer these questions in your journal.

1. *Would you like to be an archeologist and go on digs to explore and discover fossils? Why or why not?*

2. *Why do you think it's important that scientists study fossils?*

40   NATURE ANATOMY ACTIVITIES FOR KIDS

LESSON

LANDFORMS AND LANDSCAPES

The crust of our Earth is made up of many peaks and valleys, which we call landforms. Landforms are key features of our landscapes, and they can be found on continents and in the ocean. They are formed by natural forces, such as tectonic movement and erosion. Let's take a closer look at some common landforms.

Some landforms create various kinds of peaks, including the following:

Cliffs, the faces of rock that are sheer, overhanging, or vertical

Hills, rolling in appearance and smaller in height than mountains

Mid-ocean ridges, undersea mountain ranges

Mountains, areas of land that are elevated, often abruptly

Plateaus, high, flat surfaces

LESSON

Ridges, the steep edges of hills or mountains that are continuous, long, and narrow

Volcanoes, openings in Earth's crust that can expel steam, gas, ashes, and even lava

Some landforms create various kinds of valleys, including the following:

Basins, areas of land that are lower than the surrounding land

Box canyons with walls on three sides

Canyons, deep cracks into earth with walls rising up on both sides

Gullies, eroded landforms caused by running water

Ocean basins that are under seawater

Ravines, narrow canyons created by bank erosion

Valleys, also known as dales, low spots between two higher land masses

Landscape is a word we use to describe all the visible features of the land that surrounds us, including features, landforms, and plants. A desert is a type of natural landscape, whereas a city skyline is a type of a man-made landscape.

Over time, both landforms and landscapes can change. Weather such as ice, rain, and wind can cause changes, as can changes in trees and plants, and the building or destruction of man-made features. Many changes to landforms are gradual, becoming noticeable only after several years to several thousands years.

Fun Fact

DID YOU KNOW THAT ANTARCTICA IS A DESERT?

A desert is any area that receives very little precipitation, so even though Antarctica has a lot of snow, ice, and oceanwater, it receives little rain, making it a "cold desert."

ACTIVITY

CREATE YOUR OWN MINI LANDSCAPE

TIME:
1 OR MORE HOURS

CATEGORY:
CRAFTS, OUTDOOR

MATERIALS
COLLECTION OF NATURAL MATERIALS, SUCH AS STICKS, MOSS, CLAY OR OTHER SOIL, ROCKS, SHELLS, ACORNS, ETC.

AREA TO BUILD YOUR LANDSCAPE

GARDEN HAND TOOLS, SUCH AS A TROWEL

BUCKET, FOR MIXING

WATER

TIP

→ Try creating a landscape in a large shallow flowerpot on a balcony or tabletop. The same principles apply, just scale them down to fit the area you have to work in. Gather materials from a friend's house, nearby park, conservation area, or other wild space. Be sure to get permission first!

Are you drawn to a particular landscape? If you live on the plains, perhaps you wish you could see the mountains occasionally. Or maybe you live in the mountains and like how the desert looks, complete with sand and cacti. In this activity, create your dream landscape in a cozy spot in your backyard (or the yard of a friend or family member) using natural materials you can find outside along with easy-to-find materials like sand and gravel.

PREP WORK

1. Scout out an area that would make a great backdrop for your landscape scene. Roots of a tree often create little pockets that are perfect for building mountains with waterfalls. Fallen tree logs work well, too.

2. Decide what kind of landscape you want to build. Observe the shape of the location and the materials you have gathered.

3. Ask yourself what type of landscape you could create with the materials you have on hand. Do you need any additional materials, such as sand or gravel?

INSTRUCTIONS

1. Using the garden hand tools, scrape away any debris that will not fit into your landscape.

2. If you want to build up some mountains, hills, or plateaus, add some soil and water to your bucket. Add enough water to make a moldable mud.

3. Place the mud where you want it and begin sculpting it with the garden tools.

THE GROUND BENEATH US 43

ACTIVITY

4. Continue building your landscape, adding small branches for trees, moss for grass, bits of dried grass, and more to create the landscape you've imagined.

5. Can you build a log house or a fence out of sticks? Vines can often be twisted together to make an archway. Flat rocks make great pavers and pathways.

6. Dig out a stream or lake, or create a canyon in your landscape if you'd like. Continue building your landscape until you're happy with it.

7. When you're finished, document your landscape in your journal: Describe what it looks like, draw a sketch, or paste in a photo. Do any combination of things to detail the landscape in your journal.

CONCLUSION:

You imagined a landscape you wanted to create and explored different ways of creating that landscape. Just as the possibilities are endless in our world's landscapes, so are the possibilities in creating your own version.

NATURE JOURNAL ENTRY

You learned about landforms and how they help form landscapes. Summarize how you created your landscape, and think about what you've learned in this lesson. Answer the following questions in your journal.

1. *Look around where you live. Can you describe the landforms that appear in your own landscape?*

2. *What changes have you noticed in your landscape since you've lived there?*

3. *What landscape did you choose to make for your miniature landscape and why?*

NATURE ANATOMY ACTIVITIES FOR KIDS

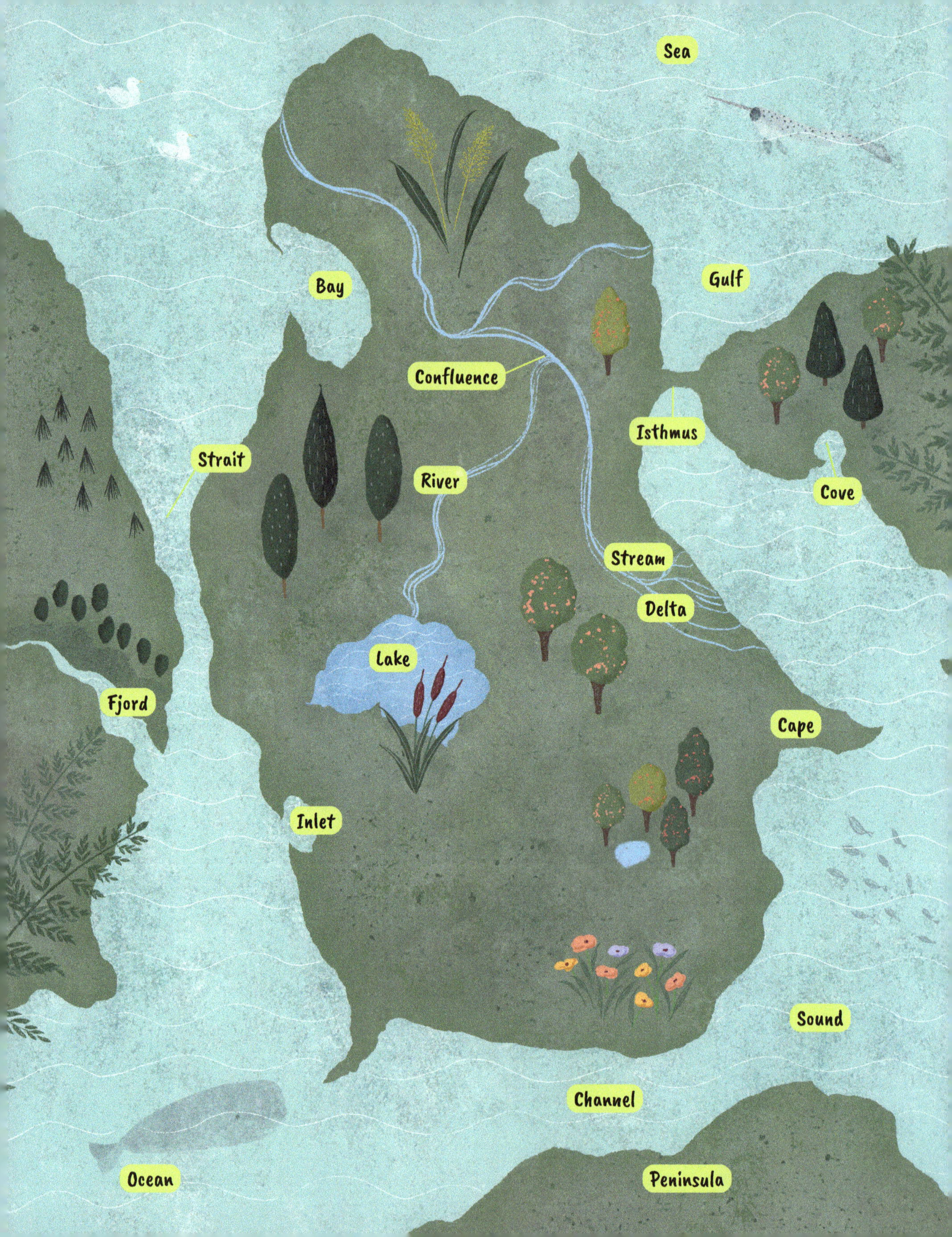
Sea
Bay
Gulf
Confluence
Isthmus
Strait
River
Cove
Stream
Delta
Lake
Fjord
Cape
Inlet
Sound
Channel
Ocean
Peninsula

THE WATER THAT SURROUNDS US

3

When you think of water, what comes to mind? Perhaps a babbling brook that meanders through a nearby park, inviting you to jump in and catch tadpoles. Or the ocean, with its waves breaking on the shore, washing up seashells and seaweed on occasion. Or maybe you picture a serene lake you've boated on with your grandfather, the two of you fishing over the boat's edge.

The following lessons focus on the water that surrounds us on Earth. These four lessons will teach you about the differences between fresh and salt water and about the ecosystems that thrive in both environments. Many of your questions about water will be answered as you work through the lessons and activities.

LESSON

BODIES OF WATER

When you think of all the bodies of water that exist in the world, you may start to realize that there are many kinds. How many can you think of?

Some bodies of water are fresh water and some are salt water. They can take many forms, including the following:

Bays, coastal bodies of water that are recessed into land and connect to a larger body of water

Bogs, spongey, cold-climate wetlands containing peat and moss

Cataracts, large or high waterfalls

Creeks, small bodies of natural running water that are bigger than streams but smaller than rivers

Lakes, either man-made or natural bodies of water that often fill a basin or other land depression

Marshes, freshwater or saltwater wetlands that support small plants, such as grasses, rushes, and sedges

Oceans, bodies of saltwater that cover much of Earth

Ponds, man-made or natural bodies of water that are smaller than lakes

Rivers, natural bodies of flowing water that run into another river, a lake, or an ocean

Seas, partially or fully landlocked places where the ocean and land meet

Sounds, inlets of seawater that are diverted and protected from the sea by land

Streams, the smallest bodies of natural running water

Swamps, wetlands that can support woody plants, like trees and shrubs

Waterfalls, bodies of water that fall over cliffs to create cascades of water

LESSON

Explorers used large bodies of water to travel all around the world, so they could explore new lands. Many people who live near the ocean rely on it for their livelihood and main source of food. Water from lakes, seas, and other bodies is continually evaporating into the air, which then becomes rainfall to water the plants on Earth. Our own bodies, which are mostly water, need constant replenishing as well, so water goes toward keeping us, and all other animals on this planet, hydrated.

Bodies of water also create natural borders for landscapes; they frame continents, countries, states, and even cities with their edges. Think about the body of water closest to your home. Does it create a natural border? Perhaps you live next to a river that separates two states or provinces. Or maybe you live near a large lake that creates a border between two countries. Or perhaps you live close to an ocean that separates two continents. Take a moment to describe this body of water in your journal.

Fun Fact

DID YOU KNOW THAT THE MAJORITY OF OUR PLANET IS COVERED IN WATER?

In chapter 2, you learned that oceans cover 60 percent of Earth. When you add in all the other bodies of water, more than 71 percent of Earth is covered in water. That's a lot of water!

ACTIVITY

BODIES OF WATER OBSERVATION

TIME:
A FEW MINUTES OVER A COUPLE WEEKS

CATEGORY:
OBSERVATION, OUTDOOR

MATERIALS
LOCAL BODIES OF WATER

TIPS

→ This activity can be an ongoing project for you as you and your family venture around your community. You may want to extend this project six months or a year, picking it back up as you visit new bodies of water.

→ Check Google Maps to view the bodies of water in your community and how they connect to one another for an even better visualization of the waterways in your area.

Do you notice the bodies of water all around you? From mud puddles in your neighborhood to the river you might cross over to get to the next town, bodies of water are everywhere. Think about the sources of these bodies (for example, rainfall creates puddles or a river feeds into a local lake) and how sustainable they are. For instance, will the mud puddle always remain in your neighborhood, or is it seasonal and dependent on regular rainfall? Does the puddle dry up for extended periods? This activity helps you think like a scientist, collect data, and compare the results.

PREP WORK

1. In your journal, make a list of all the bodies of water in your area within a short distance. Have an adult help you brainstorm if you're having trouble remembering them.

2. Make a list in your journal with six columns. Column 1 should be labeled "Body of Water"; column 2, "Location"; column 3, "Source of Water"; column 4, "Sustainability (Year-Round, Seasonal, Precipitation Dependent)"; column 5, "Type of Water (Fresh or Salt)"; and column 6, "Miscellaneous Notes."

INSTRUCTIONS

1. Over the next couple weeks, start charting bodies of water that exist in your area as you visit them.

2. As you visit each one, observe them closely. Ask yourself questions about how they got there (natural or

man-made), what the source of their water is (precipitation, overflow, ocean), if they contain water year-round or seasonally, and if they are fresh or salt water.

3. After you've compiled your list, take some time to look it over. Imagine you are in a helicopter flying overhead, can you see how any of these bodies of water are connected? How do they relate to one another (if they do)?

4. How does your community use these bodies of water? Take a few moments to think about the things these bodies of water provide for your community.

CONCLUSION:

You just explored the bodies of water that exist in your landscape and how they are used in your community. Your exploration should have given you an idea of the wide range of bodies of water not only in your landscape but also on Earth. This activity encouraged you to think scientifically about the bodies of water in your area.

NATURE JOURNAL ENTRY

Take a moment to write down what you learned exploring the different bodies of water. Consider the roles of these bodies of water on Earth. Once you've reflected on the activity, answer the following questions in your journal.

1. *Can you think of other ways water is important to us and our Earth?*

2. *How are the bodies of water in your area important to your community?*

3. *What would happen if the water source was removed for one of these bodies?*

4. *Would the other water sources be able to compensate for the missing source?*

THE WATER THAT SURROUNDS US

LESSON

FRESH WATER AND SALT WATER

Now that you've explored different bodies of water, let's zoom in a bit closer to learn about the two types of water: fresh water and salt water. Fresh water refers to lakes, rivers, streams, ponds, and rainwater, whereas salt water refers to the oceans and seas. So, how are they different from each other?

There's a clue in their names: Fresh water indicates that the water is fresh, whereas salt water indicates the water has salt. Though both waters do contain salt, there's not enough salt in fresh water to make it salty. You can drink fresh water without any problem, but if you tried to drink salt water, you would become dehydrated.

Where does this salt come from? Scientists believe that some of the salt comes from the fresh water rivers that pour into the ocean and some seeps out from the ocean floor.

Fresh water and salt water also differ in density. Density refers to the weight of the water. It might surprise you, but salt water is heavier than fresh water. If you were to weigh a cup of fresh water and a cup of salt water, the difference in weight would be noticeable.

The amount of salt in water also affects its ability to freeze. Fresh water freezes at 32 degrees Fahrenheit, but salt water must drop to 28.4 degrees Fahrenheit before it will freeze.

There is one more type of water, a mixture of fresh and salt water, called brackish water. Brackish water is found where fresh water meets salt water, such as a river flowing into an ocean. Can you think of any places where brackish water might occur?

Fun Fact

DID YOU KNOW THAT YOU CAN USE SALT WATER TO PRESERVE FOOD?

Although you can't drink salt water, a traditional method of preserving food is by using a brine, or saltwater solution. The salt water is mixed with vegetables such as cucumbers or cabbages to make pickles and sauerkraut.

ACTIVITY

FRESH WATER VERSUS SALT WATER

TIME: 30 MINUTES

CATEGORY: EXPERIMENT, INDOOR

MATERIALS
CLEAR GLASSES (2)
WATER (16 OUNCES)
TABLE SALT (5 TABLESPOONS)
EGGS (2)

Have you ever tried to float in a swimming pool but just couldn't, only to go to the ocean and float without a problem? This is because salt water is denser than fresh water, making you more buoyant. In this activity, you will prove that salt water is denser than fresh water using simple household items found in your kitchen.

TIPS

→ If you have access to ocean water, you can collect it to use in this activity instead of making your own salt water.

→ If you'd like, you can compare the weight of each glass to determine the difference in weight between the fresh water and the salt water. Which one weighed more?

PREP WORK

1. Set out the glasses and add 8 ounces of water to each glass.

2. In one of the glasses, add the salt and stir until completely dissolved.

THE WATER THAT SURROUNDS US

ACTIVITY

INSTRUCTIONS

1. What do you think will happen when you add an egg to each glass of water? Will it sink or float? Write down your hypothesis, or guess, for each glass in your journal.

2. Carefully place one egg into the freshwater glass. What happens?

3. Now, place the second egg into the saltwater glass. What happens?

4. Observe the two glasses of water with the eggs. Did the results end up being as you imagined they would?

NATURE JOURNAL ENTRY

You can't drink salt water, but you can float in it. Take some time to reflect on what you've learned, and answer any of the outstanding questions from the lesson and activity in your journal. When you're done, tackle these questions on the differences between fresh water and salt water in your journal.

1. *What happens to salt when it is stirred into a glass of fresh water?*

2. *Why is salt water denser than fresh water?*

3. *Why would an egg in brackish water not float to the top of the glass?*

CONCLUSION:

By adding salt to a glass of fresh water to create salt water, you proved that salt water is denser than fresh water. Just as you learned in the lesson, objects tend to float in water that is denser.

TIP

→ You can expand this experiment to include brackish water. Fill a third glass with 4 ounces of water and add 2½ tablespoons of table salt, stirring to dissolve. Add an egg; it should float. If it does not, add another ½ tablespoon of salt and stir to dissolve. Once the egg is floating, add 4 ounces of fresh water to the glass. The egg should hover in the middle of the glass.

NATURE ANATOMY ACTIVITIES FOR KIDS

LESSON

WATER ECOSYSTEMS

Bodies of both fresh and marine (salt) water contain ecosystems, a community in which living organisms interact with nonliving factors to create an environment that supports life. In most water ecosystems, there are plants, animals, bacteria, and fungi, as well as soil and water. Every organism within the ecosystem has a role in the community, which helps the system to survive and thrive.

Many types of freshwater ecosystems exist, including ponds, lakes, rivers, and streams. Most freshwater ecosystems have three groups that keep them healthy: producers, consumers, and decomposers. Let's take a look at these groups in a freshwater pond.

Producers. A producer changes energy from the sun and nutrients from the environment into food that can be eaten by others in the ecosystem. Producers are the basic source of food that consumers eat. In a freshwater pond, plants (such as duckweed and others) are producers.

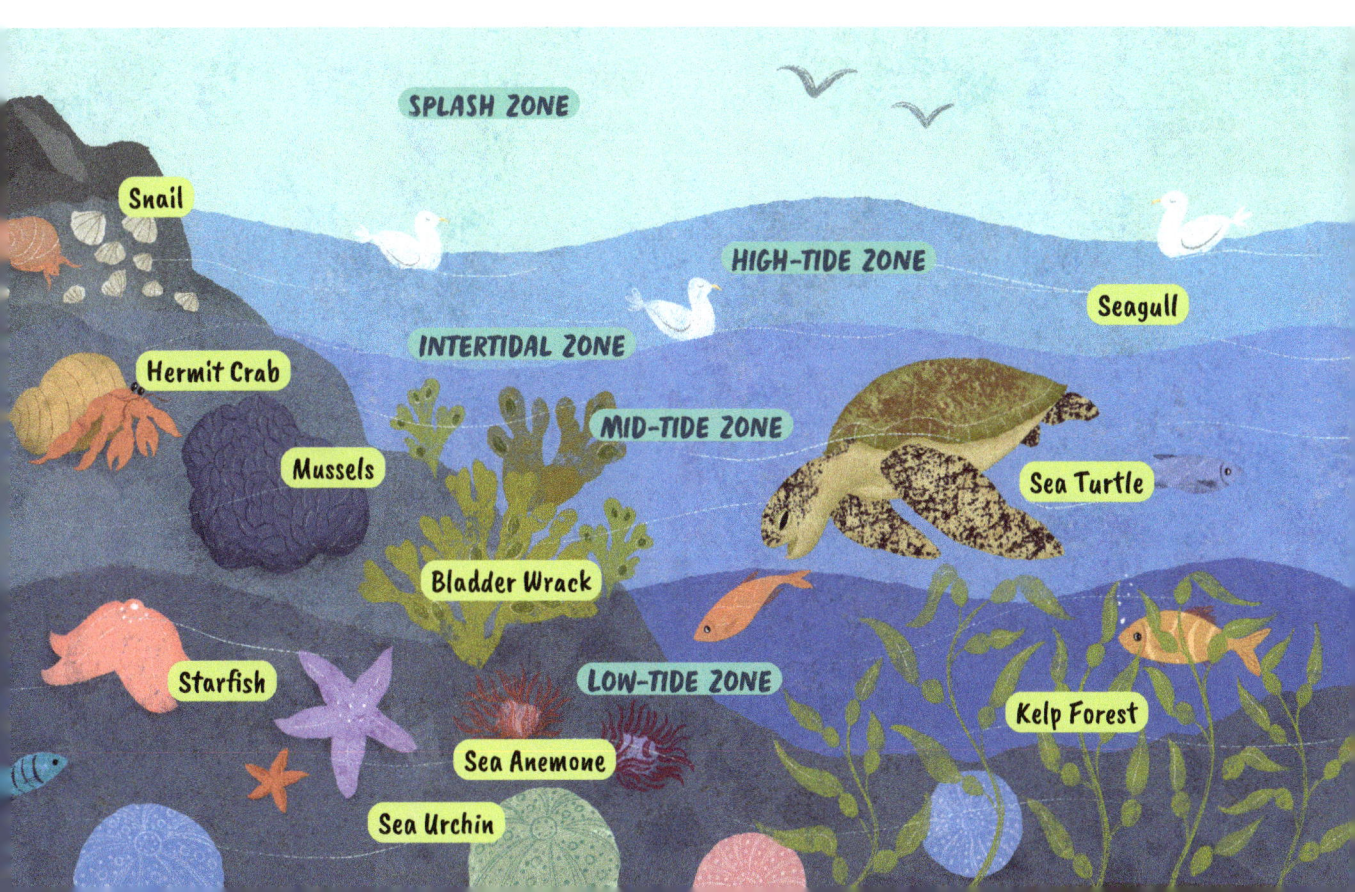

SPLASH ZONE
HIGH-TIDE ZONE
INTERTIDAL ZONE
MID-TIDE ZONE
LOW-TIDE ZONE

Snail
Hermit Crab
Mussels
Bladder Wrack
Starfish
Sea Anemone
Sea Urchin
Seagull
Sea Turtle
Kelp Forest

LESSON

Consumers. A consumer is an animal that feeds on (consumes) smaller animals and plants in the ecosystem. Fish, frogs, and herons are all consumers.

Decomposers. Decomposers help break down (decompose) decaying plants and animals. They release nutrients back into the system for producers to use for energy. Bacteria and fungi are decomposers in a pond ecosystem.

Many types of marine ecosystems exist: marshes, coral reefs, the sea floor, tidal zones, and more. Tidal zone ecosystems exist in the space between low and high tides in the ocean. The three main zones are the splash zone, the intertidal zone (which contains both the high-tide and the mid-tide zones), and the low-tide zone. Let's take a closer look.

Splash zone. The splash zone is the area beyond the high tide. Water from high tide occasionally splashes into this zone, making the area salty, but otherwise the area remains dry. Crabs, snails, barnacles, oysters, green algae, cyanobacteria, and seagulls live in the splash zone.

Intertidal zone. This zone is between the high and low tide zones where the ocean and land meet. It can be a hard zone for organisms to survive in. Waves can disrupt organisms that are attached to rocks and other surfaces. The water temperature can range from extremely hot to extremely cold. Some organisms in this zone are barnacles, limpets, crabs, mussels, shrimp, bladder wrack, toothed wrack, and spiral wrack.

Low-tide zone. The low-tide zone is always submerged in water, unlike the other zones. This area is below the turbulent wave action, offering a refuge for the organisms, including kelp, anemone, sea stars, sponges, sea urchins, and sea cucumbers, that live in this zone.

Fun Fact

DID YOU KNOW THAT MORE THAN HALF OF ALL THE SPECIES ON EARTH ARE FOUND IN MARINE ECOSYSTEMS?

Some one million species live in these watery environments.

ACTIVITY

BUILD A MINIATURE ECOSYSTEM

TIME:
1 HOUR, PLUS WAITING TIME

CATEGORY:
EXPERIMENT, INDOOR/OUTDOOR

MATERIALS
GLASS CONTAINER, SUCH AS A FISHBOWL OR A GALLON MASON JAR WITH A LID

POND WATER OR FILTERED WATER

MARKER

MUD FROM A LOCAL POND OR A SUBSTRATE FROM AN AQUATIC STORE

SAND

GRAVEL

LEAFY UNDERWATER PLANTS FROM A POND OR STORE (3 TO 4)

LARGE ROCKS (2 TO 3, OPTIONAL)

SNAILS FROM A POND OR AQUATIC STORE (2 TO 3)

CHEESECLOTH, IF USING A FISHBOWL

RUBBER BAND THAT FITS AROUND THE OPENING OF THE FISHBOWL, IF USING A FISHBOWL

TIP

➜ Collect materials from only one pond or stream.

Create a water ecosystem that will be self-sustaining for years with some maintenance. Collect your materials from a pond or stream, so you have a ready source of bacteria, though you can start from scratch. If you are starting without a pond or stream source, pay attention to the ecosystem until it can balance itself.

PREP WORK

1. Collect all your materials. Think about the layers in a pond and observe the pond you are collecting your materials from. Write down any details in your journal.

2. Wash the container with soap and water. Let it dry.

3. If you're using filtered water, let it sit out for 2 to 3 days before using, so the chlorine evaporates.

INSTRUCTIONS

1. Use the marker to mark one-quarter of the way up from the bottom of your container to give yourself a guideline for filling.

2. Add the mud or substrate first, filling the area about halfway to your mark.

3. Add a thin layer of sand to cover the mud. The sand will help keep your ecosystem a bit cleaner.

4. Add the gravel to fill the container to your mark.

5. Use your finger to carefully poke holes into the bottom layer and place plants in the holes.

THE WATER THAT SURROUNDS US

ACTIVITY

6. Divide the remaining space into three parts. Mark the first part from the top down. This is your water fill line.

7. Carefully pour the water into the container.

8. Once your water reaches the fill line, add your snails! Gently place them at the bottom.

9. If you'd like, add a few larger rocks for decoration.

10. If you're using a fishbowl, secure the cheesecloth over the top of your ecosystem with the rubber band. Otherwise, put the lid on your container.

11. Set your ecosystem in a bright location out of direct sunlight.

12. Monitor your ecosystem. If the plants look unhealthy or the water starts to cloud, move it closer to sunlight. If you start getting algae, you have too much sunlight, so move it away from the light source. Algae can also mean that you need to add more snails.

CONCLUSION:

By creating and maintaining an ecosystem, you observed how an environment needs to maintain a delicate balance to thrive. You proved that a freshwater ecosystem needs producers, consumers, and decomposers to create a healthy system.

TIP

→ You can combine pond or stream materials with items from an aquatic store. Just be sure to acclimate the animals to your ecosystem.

NATURE JOURNAL ENTRY

Write down your experiences doing this activity in your journal. Even if your ecosystem didn't thrive, valuable lessons can be learned. Answer the following questions to think a bit deeper about water ecosystems.

1. *Was maintaining an ecosystem easier or harder than you thought it would be? Why?*

2. *If you were to create a marine ecosystem, do you think it would be easier or harder to maintain than a freshwater system? Why?*

BIG AND SMALL WATER CREATURES

Let's learn about the creatures that live in both freshwater and marine ecosystems.

Among the species that live in freshwater ecosystems are many types of fish, water bugs, and frogs. To live in freshwater, creatures need to spend a lot—or all!—of their time underwater. For fish, that means being able to breathe and move underwater. Instead of lungs, fish have gills that filter water and collect the oxygen before sending the water back into the ecosystem. Fish also have a variety of fins to propel them, keep them upright, and keep them below the surface of the water. Freshwater fish include largemouth bass, bluegill, yellow perch, lake trout, green sunfish, and channel catfish.

Water bugs often skim the surface of the water, but they sometimes live below the surface. Many water bugs have legs. Examples of water bugs include water striders, damselflies, dragonflies, water boatman bugs, mosquito larvae, diving beetles, may fly larvae, and whirligigs.

Frogs are common in freshwater ecosystems. They start their life inside eggs and hatch as fish-like creatures called tadpoles, complete with a fin-like tail and gills. As tadpoles mature through a process called metamorphosis, they lose their tail and develop lungs, so they can live on land. Because they can also breathe through their skin, they can stay underwater for a long time!

Many species of fish, including parrot fish, pipe fish, puffer fish, seahorses, sharks, tuna, and swordfish, live in marine ecosystems. Marine fish are adapted to live in salt water. Most saltwater fish cannot live in fresh water and vice versa.

On the coastline, many species, including crabs, mussels, oysters, limpets, barnacles, and snails live in and out of the water. Like fish, their bodies have adapted to life on water and sand. They have legs for quick movement and shells to protect them from predators. Most of them also have gills, requiring them to spend part of their life in water.

Fun Fact

Jellyfish are not really fish. They have no brain, heart, eyes, or bones, and they shoot a stream of water for propulsion.

ACTIVITY

RAISE A TADPOLE

TIME:
30 MINUTES, PLUS 3 TO 6 WEEKS FOR LIFE CYCLE COMPLETION

CATEGORY:
EXPERIMENT, INDOOR

MATERIALS
GLASS CONTAINER, SUCH AS A FISHBOWL OR A GALLON MASON JAR

POND WATER OR FILTERED WATER

MARKER

MUD FROM A LOCAL POND OR A SUBSTRATE

SAND

GRAVEL

LEAFY UNDERWATER PLANTS FROM A POND OR AQUATIC STORE (3 TO 4)

CHEESECLOTH (OPTIONAL)

ROCK BIG ENOUGH TO STICK OUT OF THE WATER

TADPOLES OR FROG OR TOAD EGGS FROM A POND

MAGNIFYING GLASS

TADPOLE FOOD OR BOILED SPINACH

Frogs and toads begin their life in the water as tadpoles. As they become adults, they can move onto land, though some prefer to remain in the water. In this activity, you'll raise tadpoles to adulthood.

PREP WORK

1. Set up your habitat in the same manner as the Build a Miniature Ecosystem activity (see page 57), then add the large rock so it sticks out of the water. Don't cover your container with a lid, but if you'd like to keep other creatures out, use the cheesecloth to cover the top. The snails and tadpoles can live together, but you don't need the snails if you don't have them already!

2. Collect the tadpoles from the same source as the water and mud and add them to your habitat.

INSTRUCTIONS

1. Be sure to store your habitat out of direct sunlight.

2. Once your tadpoles are settled in, take time to observe them. Use the magnifying glass to look at them up close. Sketch what they look like in your journal.

3. Add a sketch to your journal of what you imagine they'll look like when they're grown up.

4. Every day, note any changes, and add a new sketch. Try to guess and imagine what type of growth will happen next, then compare your notes with the next stage of development. You might also find it fun to guess when the next stage will happen. Will it be a few days? A few weeks?

Early Stage Tadpoles

Eggs

Late Stage Tadpoles

Adult Frog

5. Be sure to feed your tadpoles with either tadpole food or a few pinches of boiled spinach.

6. Change your water weekly by removing two-thirds of the water and replacing it with either more pond water or filtered water that has been sitting for 2 to 3 days.

7. Once your frogs or toads have matured, release them back into the environment you collected them from.

NATURE JOURNAL ENTRY

You've learned about some of the many creatures that live in freshwater and marine ecosystems. You watched a frog or toad grow from a tadpole into a mature amphibian. Write your thoughts about this experience in your journal. Use these questions to help you think about your experience.

1. *What was the biggest surprise about raising your tadpoles?*

2. *What is your favorite freshwater creature and why?*

3. *What is your favorite marine creature and why?*

CONCLUSION:
Frogs and toads make up a good part of freshwater ecosystems. By raising tadpoles to frogs or toads, you observed their life cycle and watched them grow from a fish-like creature with gills into a mature frog or toad with lungs.

TIPS

➤ Make sure the tadpoles, water, and mud all come from the same pond.

➤ If your water is getting dirty really fast, cut back on the amount of food you're feeding your tadpoles.

➤ If you don't have access to tadpoles or frog or toad eggs, look online for a tadpole kit (see Resources, page 95).

THE WATER THAT SURROUNDS US   61

The Anatomy of a TREE

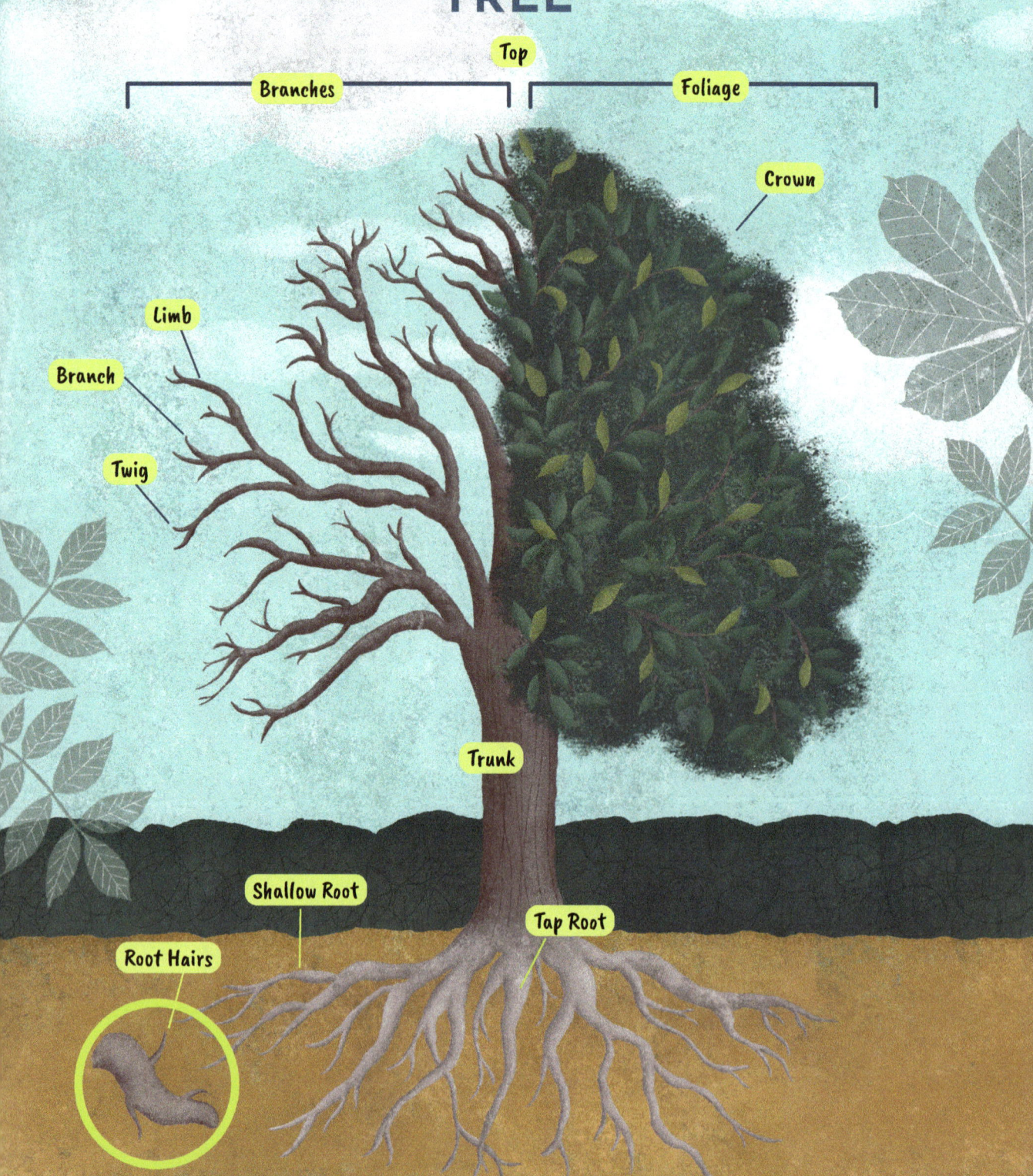

- Top
- Branches
- Foliage
- Crown
- Limb
- Branch
- Twig
- Trunk
- Shallow Root
- Tap Root
- Root Hairs

THE PLANTS IN BETWEEN

4

Go outside and look around at the plants that grow in your neighborhood. What do you see? When you look up, do you see the tops of trees? At eye level, are there a variety of bushes? What grows down around your feet? At first glance, you may see a lot of green, but when you look closely, you'll notice leaf patterns, color variations, and different textures. Trees, shrubs, flowers, mosses, and even mushrooms dot the landscape around you.

This chapter focuses on the plants that fill the landscapes of our world. You'll learn about the plants that grow on Earth and inspire your inner botanist through a variety of lessons and activities.

LESSON

White Ash Leaves

Horse Chestnut Leaves

White Oak Leaf

TREES AND LEAVES

Can you think of anything better than sitting under a tree, leaning against the trunk, and feeling the bark against your back? When you look up, all you see is a canopy of branches covered in leaves. Trees are the gentle giants of the plant world, providing shelter, lumber, food, medicine, textiles, and erosion control.

Think about the shape of trees. What keeps them standing when they grow so tall and their crowns grow so wide? Let's take a closer look at the anatomy of a tree.

Roots. Underground, a massive root system exists. Roots start out as large taproots, sinking deep into the earth, often as far down as the tree is tall. To support the tree, shallower side roots grow outward to the width of the tree's branches. Tiny root hairs emerge from the tips of the roots, which absorb water and nutrients from the soil.

Trunk. From a tree's roots grows a strong trunk that supports the tree. The trunk is covered with protective bark. The sap, a tree's blood, flows from the roots, up the trunk, and to the branches, bringing nutrients to and from the roots and leaves.

Limbs, branches, and twigs. Limbs emerge from the trunk, which give way to smaller branches that fork out into twigs.

Foliage. Foliage, the leaves of a tree, grows on branches and twigs.

Crown. The top of the tree is called the crown.

LESSON

There are two main categories of trees: deciduous (often called broadleaf) and conifer (often called evergreen).

Deciduous trees lose their leaves at the end of their growing season (usually in the fall), then resprout them at the beginning of their next growing season (usually in the spring). Leaves are used to collect sunlight, rainwater, and air to help the tree make food.

When temperatures start dropping, trees actively shed their leaves to prepare themselves for cold weather, sealing off their branches from the cold temperatures and dry air. Because winters are generally drier, trees can't get enough water to replace what they lose through their leaves, so they shed their leaves to protect themselves from water loss. This occurs during a drought, too. Deciduous trees include maple, oak, cottonwood, walnut, apple, hawthorn, birch, ash, chesnut, gingko, elm, and aspen.

The word *conifer* means "to bear cones." Unlike deciduous trees, conifers keep their foliage year-round. Instead of broadleaves, conifers have needle-like or scale-like leaves that are designed to prevent water loss, so conifers don't have to shed all their needles in the winter. Conifers do shed some of their leaves, though this process often takes place in the spring.

About 200 species of conifers grow in North America and more than 500 grow worldwide. Some common conifers are juniper, cedar, arborvitae, pine, spruce, fir, cypress, hemlock, larch, and redwood.

Eastern Pine Needles

Douglas Fir Needles

Cottonwood Leaf

THE PLANTS IN BETWEEN

LESSON

Ginko Leaf

Elm Leaf

Maple Leaf

You can quickly determine if a tree is a deciduous or conifer by looking at their leaves or needles, but you can also examine the shape and arrangement of their leaves. Conifer trees have a variety of needles that can be round, triangular, or flat, which helps you determine the type of tree. The number of needles in a "bundle," or grouping, can also determine species.

Broadleaf trees have a variety of leaf shapes. If you examine the shape of a tree's leaves, along with its fruits and bark, you can determine different trees easily, though some species can be a bit harder to identify.

The age of a tree is determined by the number of rings that radiate out from the center of the trunk. Unfortunately, a tree has to be cut down to count the number of rings. Each ring on a tree marks a year's worth of growth and reveals its history. Some years, the rings are thicker than others, which provides evidence of droughts, floods, and other weather occurrences in the tree's history.

Fun Fact

DID YOU KNOW THAT THE BERRIES OF A JUNIPER TREE ARE ACTUALLY TINY CONES?

The scales are fused together, giving the cone a berry-like appearance.

NATURE ANATOMY ACTIVITIES FOR KIDS

ACTIVITY

BROADLEAVES VERSUS EVERGREENS

TIME:
ABOUT 30 MINUTES

CATEGORY:
OBSERVATION, OUTDOOR

MATERIALS
AREA THAT HAS A VARIETY OF TREES
CRAYON
PIECE OF STRING (60 INCHES)
TAPE MEASURE OR RULER

What kinds of trees grow in your backyard or neighborhood? Do you have both deciduous (broadleaf) and conifer (evergreen) trees growing? Why do you think each type is planted? Which kind of habitat does each tree offer to the wildlife in your area? Take a walk around your backyard or neighborhood to see how many of each type of tree grows near you. This activity will help you note the differences between the two types of trees and observe their growing patterns.

PREP WORK

1. Decide the area in which you will observe your trees.

2. Take a look around and estimate which type of tree—evergreen or broadleaf—you see more of based on their leaves.

3. Guess the total number of trees in the area.

INSTRUCTIONS

1. Count how many broadleaf and evergreen trees you can find, keeping a tally of each in your journal.

2. Choose three to four broadleaf trees that have different leaf shapes, and use the crayon to do a leaf rubbing in your journal. Place a leaf, bottom-side up, under a sheet of paper, and use the side of the crayon to color over the leaf, leaving the imprint of the leaf on the page.

3. Do the same with some of the needles from the evergreen trees.

TIP

➡ If you don't have a lot of trees growing in your neighborhood, look for a local park.

THE PLANTS IN BETWEEN   67

ACTIVITY

4. Compare a sapling (baby tree) to a full-grown tree of the same species. Consider how much the trunk of a tree grows each year, and compare that with the size of each trunk. With the baby sapling, you can probably wrap one hand or both hands around the trunk. With the grown tree, can you touch your hands together when hugging it?

5. After wrapping your hands around a sapling, recreate that same distance by clasping your hands together without the tree between them. Use the string to measure the distance across your hands, then use the tape measure to measure the diameter.

6. Repeat this step with the full-grown tree in mind, measuring the diameter of your arms that surrounded the tree. Compare the size difference.

7. How close were you at guessing which type of trees were more prominent in your area? How about your guess as to how many trees overall are in your area?

CONCLUSION:

Trees come in all shapes and sizes. They create habitats for birds, squirrels, raccoons, insects, and many other creatures. Some trees, such as evergreens, are secure homes for both seasonal and year-round creatures, whereas deciduous trees are better suited for summertime homes. Trees can often be identified by their leaves; however, to determine some trees, you need to examine their twigs, bark, fruits, or seeds.

NATURE JOURNAL ENTRY

You learned about the two classifications of trees, how to determine the age of trees, and why trees are so important to the environment. Reflect on the activity as you answer these questions in your journal.

1. *Did you observe any habitats in the trees?*

2. *What kinds of animals do you think live (or did you see living) in the trees?*

68 NATURE ANATOMY ACTIVITIES FOR KIDS

The Anatomy of a WILDFLOWER

- Petal
- Stigma
- Style
- Anther
- Stamen
- Filament
- Pistil
- Ovule
- Sepal
- Ovary

WILDFLOWERS

The variety of shapes and colors in a field of wildflowers creates a spectacular view. Wildflowers are generally native flowers, meaning they have always grown on the land on which they are found, and they were not introduced to an area from another location, country, or continent.

Wildflowers can vary greatly depending on the location. Wildflowers that grow on prairies, such as Echinacea, chicory, New England aster, goldenrod, ox-eye daisy, and butterfly weed, may not be found in higher altitude alpine meadows. In those locations, you might see lupines, sticky monkey

LESSON

Sticky Monkey Flower

Lupine

Echinacea

flowers, Indian paintbrush, and arnica. Woodlands host violets, trillium, jack-in-the-pulpit, and Virginia bluebells.

Most wildflowers have very similar parts. A bisexual flower has both male and female reproductive parts. Some flowers may only have male or female reproductive parts and are known as unisexual. Let's break down those parts further.

Petals. Not all flowers have petals, but most do. The flower's petals are often a vibrant color, which attracts pollinators.

Sepals. Found directly under the petals, sepals may be green or the same color as the flower petals. Sepals often protect flower buds and support the flower when it blooms.

Female reproductive parts (pistil). The female reproductive parts, known collectively as the pistil, are located in the center of the flower. At the base is the ovary, in which the ovule is located. It becomes the fruit. The ovary is attached to a long tube known as a style. There may be one style and ovary or several on a plant. The tip of the style is known as the stigma.

Male reproductive parts (stamen). The male parts generally circle the female parts on a bisexual flower. The stamen is broken into two parts: the filament, which is the stem of the stamen, and the anther, which is found at the top of the filament. The anther holds the pollen.

So why do flowers come in all shapes, sizes, and colors? Botanists, scientists who study plants, have found many reasons for these

LESSON

differences. Some flowers are capable of pollinating by the wind, so they generally do not have showy flowers, because they don't need to attract a pollinator.

Other flowers rely on insects and birds for pollination. As the insects drink the nectar, some of the pollen sticks to their legs. When they walk to another flower, the pollen may fall off, effectively pollinating the flower.

Some plants are tubular, which attracts hummingbirds. Other plants are very small, so only tiny insects can pollinate them. Bees, wasps, flies, ants, butterflies, and moths are some types of pollinators. Can you think of others?

Butterfly Weed

Violet

Chicory

Fun Fact

DID YOU KNOW THAT SOME FLOWERS ONLY POLLINATE WHEN THEY ARE BUZZED BY BEES?

If you've ever heard a bee buzzing on a flower, you've witnessed buzz pollination! The pollen on the anthers of these flowers are only released through the vibration of a bee's buzz.

THE PLANTS IN BETWEEN

ACTIVITY

Flower Watercolors

TIME:
10 MINUTES,
PLUS 1 HOUR TO STEEP

CATEGORY:
CRAFTS, INDOOR, OBSERVATION

MATERIALS
VARIETY OF COLORFUL FLOWERS, SUCH AS PURPLE, RED, ORANGE, AND YELLOW

CONTAINERS, SUCH AS 4-OUNCE JELLY JARS (3 FOR EACH FLOWER)

HOT WATER

LEMON JUICE

BAKING SODA

POPSICLE STICKS

WATERCOLOR PAPER

PAINTBRUSH

Vibrant wildflowers are pretty to look at and good to attract insects, but they also make great plant dyes! In this activity, you will collect flowers to turn into watercolor paints, which you'll use to paint a picture.

Safety First: *Be careful when pouring the boiling water.*

PREP WORK

1. Remove the petals from the flowers.

2. Split each type of flower petal into three jars, adding at least 1 tablespoon of petals to each jar.

3. Heat your water on the stove until it's boiling.

INSTRUCTIONS

1. When the water is ready, carefully pour just enough hot water on the flowers to cover them. Let them steep for about 1 hour.

2. While the petals are steeping, use your scientist skills to observe the color changes in the water. Describe the colors in your journal.

3. Now, you can start adding lemon juice (an acid) and baking soda (an alkaline) to some of the paints. What do you think will happen when they are added? Do you think they will change colors or stay the same?

4. Leave the first jar untouched. In the second jar, add a few drops of lemon juice. In the third jar, add a sprinkle of baking soda. Use a Popsicle stick to stir the contents

in each jar. What happened? Write your observations in your journal.

5. Now, you can start painting with your colors. First, you'll want to create a test strip for each color. Cut out a small piece of watercolor paper that will fit into your journal. Then dip a paintbrush in each color, one at a time, and paint a small line on the paper. Rinse your brush off between jars. Once you have all the colors painted, note the flower you used and which paints had the lemon juice and baking soda added to them. Add the test paper to your journal for future reference.

6. Finally, you're ready to paint! Use the test strip as a guide to choose your colors when painting your picture. Rinse the paintbrush with water between jars to keep your colors from getting mixed.

NATURE JOURNAL ENTRY

After you've finished recording your watercolor experiences, reflect on the lesson and activity while answering these questions.

1. *When you were steeping the flower petals, did some of the colors surprise you? If so, why?*

2. *Why do you think some flowers attract specific insects while others seem to attract all kinds of insects?*

CONCLUSION:
Wildflowers come in a variety of colors to attract pollinators. Some petals create quite vivid colors, whereas some petals make colors that are more muted.

TIPS

➡ If you don't have access to a flower garden, try collecting flowers from a wild spot. Be sure to check your local rules on plant collecting.

➡ If you purchase flowers from a florist for this activity, make sure they haven't been dyed. Sometimes florists dye flowers to make them more vibrant.

THE PLANTS IN BETWEEN

LESSON

The Anatomy of a Fern

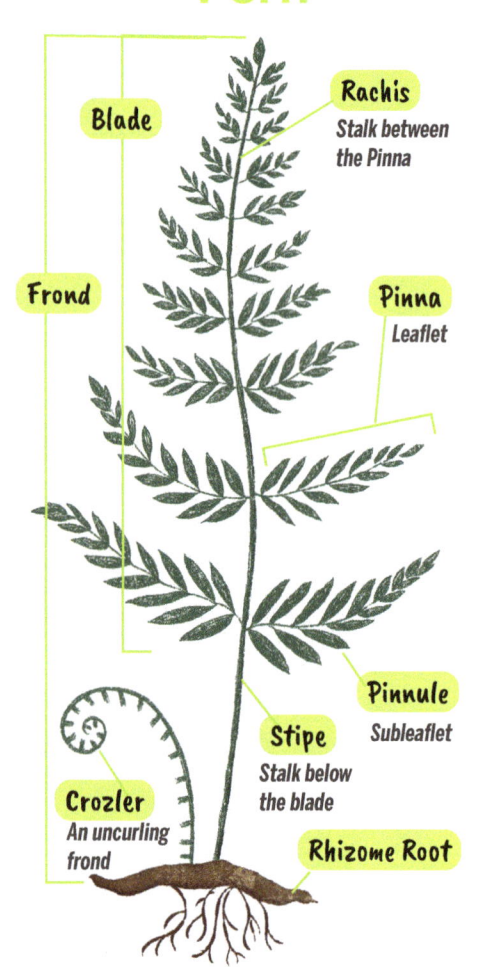

- **Blade**
- **Rachis** — Stalk between the Pinna
- **Frond**
- **Pinna** — Leaflet
- **Pinnule** — Subleaflet
- **Stipe** — Stalk below the blade
- **Crozier** — An uncurling frond
- **Rhizome Root**

MORE UNIQUE PLANTS

Plants like lichens and mushrooms are not actually plants but organisms that are classified in other kingdoms. Before this lesson explores those kingdoms, let's take a look at two plants that are unique but still in the plant kingdom: ferns and mosses.

Ferns. While ferns have stems, roots, leaves, and vascular systems, unlike many plants, ferns reproduce via spores, which are similar to seeds. Ferns prefer moist habitats and lots of shade. They come in all different sizes, from barely an inch high up to 45 feet.

Mosses. Mosses range from about ½ to 20 inches in height. They evolved from algae and lack roots, stems, flowers, and vascular tissue. They can only grow where the air quality is good, and they produce their energy through photosynthesis and reproduce through spores. Mosses need moisture to survive and go dormant during drought. They are often found in shady areas on the ground, in trees, or on rocks.

Now let's take a look at mushrooms and lichens. Though you might hear people refer to them as plants, mushrooms and lichens are really organisms from other kingdoms.

Mushrooms. Mushrooms are in the fungi kingdom. Fungi cell walls are composed of chitin instead of cellulose (as plants are) and lack chlorophyll, so they cannot

74 NATURE ANATOMY ACTIVITIES FOR KIDS

LESSON

Anthocerote Moss

Musci Moss

Hepaticae Moss

Portobello Mushroom

Portobello Mushroom Gills

photosynthesize as plants do. Other fungi include yeast, mold, mildew, and rust. Mushrooms reproduce by spores and grow from mycelium, which is the body of the mushroom. The part of the mushroom you see above ground is the fruit. In nature, mushrooms help decompose dead plant materials and are often found growing on deadfall in the woods. Though some mushrooms are highly toxic, several types of mushrooms are edible and medicinal.

Lichens. Lichens are a symbiosis, or partnership, of a fungus from the Fungi kingdom and an alga from the Protista kingdom, or sometimes a cyanobacterium from the Bacteria kingdom. The three types of lichens are crustose, foliose, and fruticose. To this day, scientists have never seen lichen reproducing! Lichens are used as antibiotics and antibacterials, dyes for clothing, nesting material for birds, and food for animals. They also break down rocky surfaces to prepare the area for trees and grasses to grow, help fertilize soil, and recycle airborne chemicals into the soil to help clean the air. Lichens usually grow on trees, stones, or the ground.

Fun Fact

DID YOU KNOW THAT MORE THAN 120,000 SPECIES OF FUNGI HAVE BEEN IDENTIFIED?

But scientists estimate there may be close to four million species in total!

THE PLANTS IN BETWEEN

ACTIVITY

Mushroom Spore Prints

Shiitake Mushroom

There are many mushroom look-alikes in nature. Sometimes, the only way to identify a mushroom is through its spore print. In this activity, you will collect some mushrooms that grow around you and create spore prints to see if you can identify the mushrooms. You'll also use Mushroom-Appreciation.com, a website that teaches people how to identify mushrooms.

Safety First: *Never put a wild mushroom in your mouth or put your hands in your mouth after touching a mushroom from the wild, since many are toxic. If you do not feel comfortable handling wild mushrooms, simply buy fresh mushrooms from the grocery store.*

TIME:
1 TO 2 HOURS, PLUS TIME TO ALLOW THE SPORE PRINTS TO DEVELOP

CATEGORY:
EXPERIMENT, INDOOR/OUTDOOR

MATERIALS
MUSHROOMS (AS MANY AS YOU WANT)
SHEET OF WAX PAPER
WHITE PAPER
BLACK OR DARK BLUE PAPER
COOKIE SHEETS (2)
HAIR SPRAY (OPTIONAL)
TISSUE PAPER (OPTIONAL)

PREP WORK

1. Collect a variety of mushrooms from your yard, local woods, park, or grocery store. You will need two of each kind. Look for fresh species, ideally with gills that are visible under the cap. This indicates they are ready to release their spores. Pored mushrooms will work, too.

2. Place the mushrooms on the wax paper, and organize them by color.

3. Place a piece of white paper on one cookie sheet and a piece of dark blue or black paper on the other cookie sheet.

ACTIVITY

INSTRUCTIONS

1. Observe all the mushrooms you have gathered. Based on the color of the mushroom, can you guess which mushrooms will have which color spore prints? Spores can range in color from white to cream to gray, brown, or black. Imagine what color each mushroom's spores will be.

2. Do a quick sketch of each mushroom in your journal, and write your guess next to each sketch.

3. Now that you've made your hypotheses, you can test them. Remove the stems from your mushrooms, and place one of each mushroom on the white paper and one of each on the dark paper.

4. Wash your hands.

5. Let your mushrooms sit for a few hours.

6. Peek at your mushrooms. Look for any dark coloration on the white paper or light coloration on the dark paper coming from under the edges of the mushroom caps.

7. After several hours, carefully remove your mushrooms and compare the results with your notes. Note the differences.

8. Head over to the Mushroom Appreciation website (see the Resources section on page 95) to try to identify your mushroom using the physical features of the mushroom and your spore prints. Write down your findings in your journal.

TIPS

→ Try your hand at growing your own mushrooms. Many mushroom kits are available for purchase online (see the Resources section on page 95).

→ Color your mushroom sketches, so they look like the actual mushrooms.

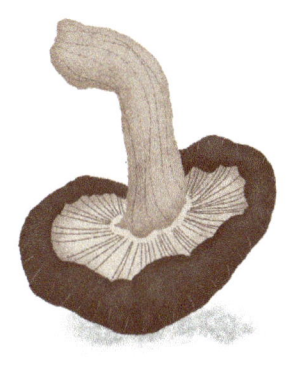

Spores of a Shiitake Mushroom

THE PLANTS IN BETWEEN

ACTIVITY

9. If you'd like to save your spore prints and add them to your journal, you can spray them with the hair spray, which will set them on the paper. For extra protection, lay a piece of tissue paper over the spore print after attaching the prints in your journal.

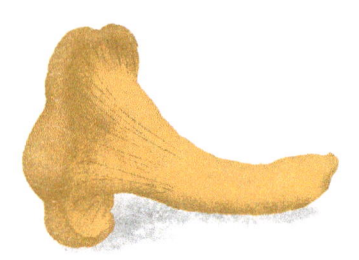

Chanterelle Mushroom

Spores of a Chanterelle Mushroom

CONCLUSION:
Some plants, like mushrooms, ferns, and mosses, reproduce by spores. You tested that theory by making spore prints of mushrooms. You can use spore prints to help you identify mushrooms.

NATURE JOURNAL ENTRY

Reflect on your activity as you answer these questions in your journal.

1. *In this activity, you had to place mushrooms on both light and dark paper to determine the color of the spores. Why do you think the spores are different colors?*

2. *Do you think spores are more effective or less effective (or the same) at reproduction than flowers, which use pollen to reproduce? Why?*

Bee
Red-tailed Hawk
Swallow
Brown Bear
Fox
Great Blue Heron
Dragonfly
Praying Mantis
Rabbits

THE CREATURES IN BETWEEN

Some creatures crawl, others hop, and others fly. In both cities and the wilderness, the world is filled with creatures big and small—from the birds that chirp, honk, and chitter, to the insects that buzz, flutter, and crawl, to the creatures that scurry, lumber, or slink.

In this chapter, you will learn all about the organisms that live on land. If you're curious about birds, animals, and insects, this is the chapter for you! You'll learn about a variety of creatures and find answers to your questions about them as you make your way through the lessons and activities.

LESSON

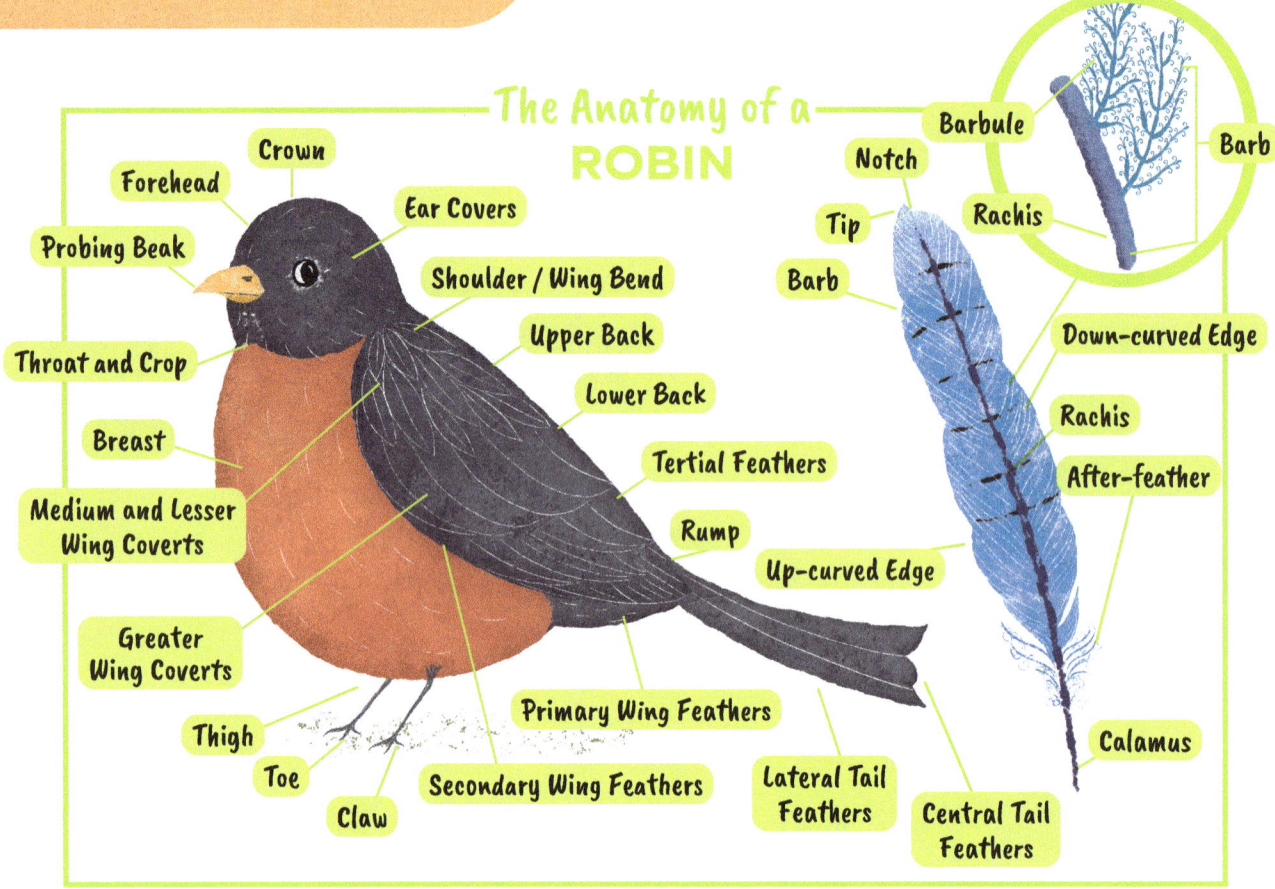

The Anatomy of a ROBIN

- Forehead
- Crown
- Ear Covers
- Probing Beak
- Shoulder / Wing Bend
- Upper Back
- Lower Back
- Throat and Crop
- Breast
- Tertial Feathers
- Medium and Lesser Wing Coverts
- Rump
- Up-curved Edge
- Greater Wing Coverts
- Thigh
- Toe
- Claw
- Primary Wing Feathers
- Secondary Wing Feathers
- Lateral Tail Feathers
- Central Tail Feathers

Feather parts:
- Notch
- Tip
- Barb
- Barbule
- Rachis
- Barb
- Down-curved Edge
- Rachis
- After-feather
- Calamus

BIRDS

Have you ever woken up to the sound of birds singing outside your window? Or spent the afternoon watching birds at the bird feeder? Some are big, such as ostriches and emus, and some are tiny, such as hummingbirds, but all birds have similar characteristics. Let's take a closer look at key parts of their anatomy.

Feathers. Instead of fur, birds are covered with feathers, which help them take flight and remain in the air. Feathers are also designed to help birds shed water, so they stay dry in the rain. Birds have six different types of feathers: flight, contour, semiplume, filoplume, bristle, and down. Feathers can be all kinds of colors, which will help you identify the bird and whether it's a juvenile or male or female.

LESSON

Wings. Birds have wings, and most species (though not all) use them to fly. After using their legs to thrust themselves into the air, birds flap their wings to lift them up into the sky. From there, the wings, which are cup-shaped, create airfoils that hold air under them to keep the bird suspended while they glide. Penguins, whose wings are better suited for helping them swim through the icy ocean, are one of the few birds that cannot fly. Ostriches, emus, and kiwis are some others that cannot fly. The wing's shape can help you identify the bird.

Hollow bones. Birds' bones are hollow, so they are lightweight. This quality gives birds an advantage when they fly.

Beaks. You can determine what a bird eats by the shape of its beak. Birds that tap into trees to catch insects have long thin beaks, whereas birds who eat seeds have shorter, thicker beaks. The shape of a bird's beak can help you identify them.

There are many types of birds. Let's look at a few groups of birds, and think about what each has in common.

Songbirds. Songbirds belong to the category of birds called Passeriformes, or perching birds. There are more than 5,000 species of songbirds! Birds in this group have developed a syrinx, or song box, which allows them to sing melodious songs. Songbirds include robins, nightingales, warblers, kinglets, sunbirds, skylarks, and sparrows. Even crows are considered songbirds, though most people wouldn't call their song melodious.

Insect-catching Beak
Swallow

Grain-eating Beak
Blue Tit

Nectar-feeding Beak
Ruby-throated Hummingbird

Chiseling Beak
Northern Flicker Woodpecker

Fruit-eating Beak
Toucan

THE CREATURES IN BETWEEN

LESSON

Red-tailed Hawk

Birds of prey. Also called raptors, birds of prey hunt other animals, which are often fairly large in comparison with the bird's own size. Birds of prey have keen eyesight, allowing them to detect food from the sky during flight; they have large talons to grip and kill their prey; and they have curved beaks that easily cut and tear flesh. Not all birds of prey eat live animals. Some, such as vultures and condors, mainly eat dead animals, called carrion. Other birds of prey include hawks, eagles, falcons, ospreys, and kites.

Water birds. Water birds, or waterfowl, are birds that live on or around water. Freshwater birds include ducks, geese, swans, egrets, cranes, and storks. Saltwater birds include seagulls, penguins, pelicans, and puffins.

Great Blue Heron

Fun Fact

DID YOU KNOW THAT CHICKENS ARE CLOSELY RELATED TO TYRANNOSAURUS REX?

Remains of a T. rex found in 2003 provided enough DNA that scientists could determine that chickens, along with ostriches, are the closest related animal to the now extinct dinosaur.

ACTIVITY

BIRDWATCHING

TIME: SHORT PERIODS OVER THE COURSE OF SEVERAL DAYS OR WEEKS

CATEGORY: OBSERVATION, OUTDOOR

MATERIALS
BIRD IDENTIFICATION BOOK FOR YOUR AREA

BINOCULARS

CELL PHONE OR ANOTHER RECORDING DEVICE (OPTIONAL)

TIPS

→ If you don't have one, set up a bird feeder in your backyard to attract birds. You can use a general bird feeder or add a few different types, such as a hummingbird feeder and a finch feeder.

→ Offer a place for birds to bathe and drink water.

What kinds of birds live in your neighborhood? In this activity, you will observe the birds that live in your neighborhood and create a record of them in your journal. The goal of this activity is to try to identify 10 birds that are in your neighborhood.

PREP WORK

1. Set up a chart in your journal that has six columns. Label them "Date Seen," "Bird," "Description," "Location," "Male/Female," and "How Many."

2. Look through your bird identification book to see if any of the birds in the book look familiar to you.

3. Find a quiet spot to sit outdoors where you can observe the birds. You might find it easier to observe birds from your window during extremely hot or cold days, but try to get outside so you can hear their songs, too.

INSTRUCTIONS

1. Observe the birds in your area, and ask yourself if you recognize any of them. You might want to make a preliminary list of birds you expect to see.

2. As you start to observe the birds in your area, make notes on your chart. Can you tell if the bird you are looking at is male or female? A good rule of thumb is that male birds are more colorful than females, which are often drab in color.

THE CREATURES IN BETWEEN

ACTIVITY

3. Use your identification book to help you identify your birds. How many of each type of bird did you see?

4. Optionally, use a cell phone to record their songs, so you can compare the different birds with their songs.

5. Over the course of several days, or even a few weeks, observe the birds in your area and add them to your list. Try to discover at least 10 different types of birds. Can you find more?

Aerial-fishing Beak
Kingfisher

CONCLUSION:

You observed many different birds. Depending on your neighborhood, you will have seen birds that fit into your location. For instance, in a city, you probably observed a lot of pigeons and sparrows, whereas in a more suburban setting, you probably saw a variety of songbirds. If you're near a body of water, you might have seen ducks, geese, or even swans. Just as you learned in the lesson, many types of birds live in our world.

NATURE JOURNAL ENTRY

After learning about the different types of birds that live on this planet, you watched and discovered birds that live in your neighborhood. Think about the birds you observed, look back at your notes, then answer these questions in your journal.

1. *Why do you think male birds are often more colorful than female birds?*

2. *Do you see birds most often in pairs or random groups? Or both?*

3. *Do the bird groups change depending on the type of bird you're watching?*

86 NATURE ANATOMY ACTIVITIES FOR KIDS

LESSON

INSECTS

Scientists estimate that between 2 million and 30 million types of insects are crawling, buzzing, and flying on Earth. Entomologists, scientists who study insects, say that more than 10 quintillion (10,000,000,000,000,000,000) insects roam Earth at any given time. That's a lot of bugs!

An insect has three bodyparts (a head, a thorax, and an abdomen), three sets of legs, and one or two pairs of wings. That description leaves out spiders, which are arachnids.

Let's take a closer look at the three body parts of insects.

Head. The first segment, the head, contains eyes (sometimes more than two), a brain, antennae, and mouthparts, which vary from insect to insect.

Thorax. The middle segment, the thorax, contains the wings and legs and attaches the head to the abdomen. The heart is located here.

Abdomen. The final segment is the abdomen. The genitalia, stomach, and rectum, are located here and often a stinger.

Which insects can be found in your neighborhood? Bees, butterflies, lightning bugs, grasshoppers, cicadas, crickets, flies, ladybugs, ants, praying mantises, mosquitos, and dragonflies are all insects. Though these insects all act differently, they share the same body characteristics.

Insects play many roles. Some help pollinate plants, as you learned in chapter 4 (page 71). Others help keep pest insects in check by eating them. Still others help clean up by feasting on decaying plants and animals.

Fun Fact
DID YOU KNOW THAT ANTS CAN CARRY OBJECTS 50 TIMES THEIR OWN WEIGHT WITH THEIR JAWS?

The Anatomy of a DRAGONFLY
- Head
- Thorax
- Abdomen

THE CREATURES IN BETWEEN

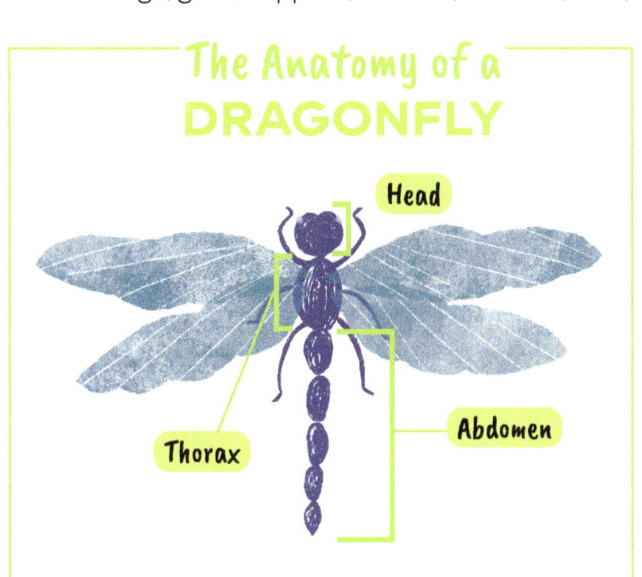

ACTIVITY

ANT-TAC-TOE

TIME:
15 TO 30 MINUTES

CATEGORY:
CRAFTS, INDOOR

MATERIALS
RULER
BLACK MARKER
SQUARE OF CARDBOARD (6-BY-6 INCHES)
NEWSPAPER
SMOOTH FLAT STONES, ABOUT THE SIZE OF A QUARTER (12)
RED ACRYLIC PAINT
PAINTBRUSH
BLACK ACRYLIC PAINT
MOD PODGE

TIPS

→ Use a small canvas bag to store the playing pieces.

→ Want to make this game a buzz-tac-toe game? Paint one set of stones as a black bee, and the other set as a yellow honeybee.

Ant-tac-toe is a modified version of tic-tac-toe that helps you remember the body parts of an insect. This activity can be modified to use any insect, but is especially clever using ants, as there are both red and black ants in the world. Can you build an ant before your opponent?

PREP WORK

1. Using the ruler and marker, create a tic-tac-toe grid on the cardboard square. Set it aside.

2. Lay down a piece of newspaper, and divide your stones into two piles of six.

3. Squirt out a bit of red paint next to your first pile. Using the paintbrush, paint two ant heads on two stones, two ant thoraxes on two stones, and two ant abdomens on two stones. Set them aside to dry.

4. Meanwhile, rinse off your paintbrush.

5. Repeat step 3 using the black paint and the remaining six stones.

6. Rinse off the paintbrush.

7. Once the stones are dry, use your paintbrush to coat them in Mod Podge. This will seal the paint onto the stones. Let them dry.

INSTRUCTIONS

1. This game takes two people to play, so challenge someone to play with you!

88 NATURE ANATOMY ACTIVITIES FOR KIDS

2. The first player puts down a head on the board. Then it's the second player's turn. They also put down a head on the board.

3. The players continue to rotate, trying to build a complete red or black ant.

4. The player who makes a complete ant wins.

Red Ants

CONCLUSION:
The bodies of ants and other insects have three parts. This game helps you remember the order of the body parts: head, thorax, then abdomen.

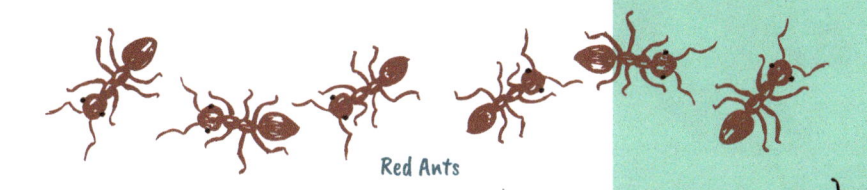

Black Ants

NATURE JOURNAL ENTRY

There's a lot to learn about insects. You learned they have three body parts, three sets of legs, and one or two sets of wings. You also learned they have many roles on Earth. Reflect back on the lesson as you answer these questions in your journal.

1. *Insects are beneficial, even if you think they're just pests. Can you think of any benefits that ants offer?*

2. *What would you do if you could lift objects that weighed 50 times as much as you?*

THE CREATURES IN BETWEEN

LESSON 6

The Anatomy of a SKUNK

- **Mostly black fur with white striping from back of head to tip of tail**
- **Ear**
- **Eye**
- **Nose**
- **Sensory Whiskers**
- **Each foot has five toes and claws**
- **Black and White Bushy Tail**
- **Back Paw Print**
- **Front Paw Print**

CREATURES INSIDE (AND OUTSIDE) YOUR NEIGHBORHOOD

Not all animals live in wild places. Many animals, such as squirrels, raccoons, and rabbits, have learned to live where people live—in cities and neighborhoods. Perhaps you've seen a few!

Though outside animals are wild, unlike the domesticated animals we keep as pets, many have learned to tolerate people because they are exposed to them every day. Outside creatures often use the spaces that humans have made as their homes. For example, woodchucks often live near gardens for easy access to tasty vegetables. Skunks like to make their homes under porches, and bats often build their homes in chimneys. As natural habitats are destroyed to put up homes and businesses for people, more animals are learning to live with humans.

Many animals you've seen during the day, such as skunks, mice, opossums, raccoons, foxes, coyotes, and bats, are nocturnal—that is, they sleep

LESSON

through the day and are active at night. If you see one of these animals during the day, chances are it's hungry and still looking for a meal. Most of these animals eat smaller animals or eggs, whereas some, such as the bat, feast on insects or eat only plants.

As you venture farther away from urban areas, you may encounter even wilder animals. Depending on your location, there may be marmots, bears, wolves, cougars, elk, moose, deer, bison, antelope, mountain goats, or bighorn sheep. These animals all coexist. In the wild, herbivores (animals that eat plants) might become a meal for carnivores (animals that eat meat), but this creates a balanced habitat. Without this balance, the herbivores would overpopulate the area, eating all the vegetation and destroying the habitat. The herbivores would then get sick when no food is left for them.

Years ago, hunting wolves became illegal in the West. As the wolf population increased, the bison, antelope, and deer populations (which had overpopulated) started to shrink until balance was restored. Today, all these animals cohabitate well.

The same is true if you live in a warmer climate, such as Florida, where alligators, panthers, turtles, manatees, snakes, capybaras, and otters live. When these animals are left alone, they maintain a balanced habitat. Generally, when people get involved and try to control animal populations, wild animals either become destructive or endangered.

Brown Bear

Fox

Fun Fact

DID YOU KNOW THAT OPOSSUMS ARE THE ONLY MARSUPIAL ANIMAL IN NORTH AMERICA?

A marsupial has a pouch to carry its babies.

THE CREATURES IN BETWEEN

ACTIVITY

NEIGHBORHOOD WILDLIFE WATCH

TIME:
SHORT PERIODS OVER THE COURSE OF SEVERAL DAYS OR WEEKS

CATEGORY:
OBSERVATION, OUTDOOR

MATERIALS
BINOCULARS (OPTIONAL)

TIP

→ If you live in a large city, you might be surprised at how many wild animals live in your neighborhood. Keep your eyes peeled and look for wild spaces, such as a local park or vacant lot.

Just how many wild animals live in urban and suburban locations may surprise you! Over the next few days or weeks, start tracking any animals you observe. Look for woodchucks hanging out by a busy roadway, or raccoons invading trash cans in the evening. Dusk is a great time to discover many nocturnal animals as they begin to wake up from their day's slumber.

PREP WORK

1. Create a chart in your journal. Make five columns and label them "Date Seen," "Animal," "Description," "Location," and "Notes."

2. Observe your neighborhood and look for wildlife hot spots.

INSTRUCTIONS

1. Start keeping a record of the animals you see. Ask yourself these questions:

- Do they travel alone, or do they travel in a group?
- Are they looking for food? If so, what do they eat?
- Am I seeing the same animal every day or different animals?

2. Over the course of the next several days or few weeks, see if you can notice 5 to 10 different wildlife animals in your neighborhood.

Deer

3. Once you've filled in your chart, think about the animals you saw. Were you surprised at the variety, or lack of, that you saw? Was one type of animal more prevalent than another? If so, why do you think that was?

Rabbit

CONCLUSION:

Many wild animals have learned to adapt to urban and suburban settings as their habitats shrink. By observing and noting the creatures in your neighborhood, you proved that many wildlife animals live in both urban and suburban areas.

TIP

→ If you're not seeing any animals at dusk, try a different time of day. Dawn is another good time to see wildlife on the move.

NATURE JOURNAL ENTRY

You learned about the habitats of urban and wild animals and how the two groups overlap. You also learned the importance of balance in a habitat to keep it healthy. Think about the creatures that live in your neighborhood and answer these questions.

1. *Based on what you've learned about wild animals in their habitats, why might animals in urban environments still be hungry during the day?*

2. *Have you ever seen a nocturnal animal out during the day? If so, what kind of animal was it and what kind of food do you think it was looking for?*

THE CREATURES IN BETWEEN

RESOURCES

BOOKS

The following books are great resources to learn more about the topics in this book.

Forest School Adventure: Outdoor Skills and Play for Children (2018). A great book written by Naomi Walmsley and Dan Westall to further explore the great outdoors with many ideas for crafts and activities.

Nature Anatomy: The Curious Parts & Pieces of the Natural World (2015) and Ocean Anatomy: The Curious Parts & Pieces of the World Under the Sea (2020). Julia Rothman has written two great companion books that cover the topics in this book in more detail and include whimsical drawings.

Play the Forest School Way: Woodland Games, Crafts, and Skills for Adventurous Kids (2016) and A Year of Forest School: Outdoor Play and Skill-building Fun for Every Season (2018). Written by Peter Houghton and Jane Worroll, these books include additional games and activities to encourage play outdoors.

Shanleya's Quest: A Botany Adventure for Kids Ages 9 to 99 (2005) and Shanleya's Quest 2: Botany Adventure at the Fallen Tree (2020). These books and card sets by Thomas J. Elpel are great for teaching botany through storytelling and games.

The Bluest of Blues: Anna Atkins and the First Book of Photographs (2019). In this book by Fiona Robinson, learn more about Anna Atkins and her desire to capture the plants all around her. Anna explores and documents her findings while being educated scientifically by her father.

The Kingfisher Science Encyclopedia (2017). Charles Taylor has written a great reference guide to dive deeper into science and natural subjects.

The Organic Artist for Kids: A DIY Guide to Making Your Own Eco-Friendly Art Supplies from Nature (2020). This book by Nick Neddo provides more explorations, crafts, and activities for creating your own art supplies from nature.

The Usborne Illustrated Dictionary of Science (2012). Written by Corinne Stockley, this book is a great reference.

JOURNALS

The following are a few of my favorite journals to use for sketching and writing. Use this list when you're looking for your nature journal.

Crafters Workshop Dylusions Dyan Reaveley's Creative Journal. This 5-by-8-inch journal is a great size for kids. Other sizes are available as well, including a square version. One disadvantage is that it doesn't have dot grids for writing guidance.

Dingbats Earth Dotted Medium A5+ Hardcover Journal. This is a standard journal that has smooth pages and is suitable for pen, colored pencils, and light markers.

Tekukor A5 Hardcover Dot Journal. This journal is great if you like to paint with watercolors. The pages are a bit thicker and can stand up to watercolor paint, marker, and colored pencil.

ONLINE

The following are a few online resources to learn more about the topics in this book and find more activities to do.

Grow-a-Frog. This is a great resource for tadpoles and activity kits. (GrowAFrog.com)

Herbal Roots zine. My website features more than 130 publications that teach children about the medicinal uses of herbs. In addition to downloadable ebooks, there are a variety of online classes that range from 30 days to one year that can be used to teach children about herbs, botany, and drawing. (HerbalRootszine.com)

Museum of Natural and Cultural History. This museum has a great webpage about the rocks and minerals on Earth. (MNCH.UOregon.edu/rocks-and-minerals-everyday-uses)

Mushroom Adventures. If you want to try your hand at growing mushrooms, lots of great kits are available on this website. Choose from portabella, cremini, white button, shiitake, and oyster mushrooms. (MushroomAdventures.com)

Mushroom Appreciation. This website is great to help you learn to identify a variety of mushrooms. Select the "Mushroom Identification" page from the "Categories" pull-down menu to get started. (Mushroom-Appreciation.com)

ACKNOWLEDGMENTS

I'd like to thank my partner, Greg, for agreeing that I stay at home and homeschool our two youngest children, which gave me the opportunity to teach fun nature topics to all our children.

I'm also grateful to my parents for raising me on a farm so that nature was a part of my everyday life. Exploring the world around me was as natural as breathing the air and it instilled in me a desire to raise my own children in the same manner.

And I'd like to thank my children for being willing participants in learning about all things natural, while tolerating my geeking out over our many nature finds. A special thanks to my daughter Adelena, the creator of the Ant-Tac-Toe game, which I used with her permission.

ABOUT THE AUTHOR

Kristine Brown, RH (AHG), is a practicing traditional community herbalist who homeschooled two of her children for 11 years. She has taught classes for homeschooled children locally and coordinated numerous kids' camps on herbalism both locally and nationally. She also assists Leslie Alexander, PhD, RH (AHG), with the American Herbalist Guild Symposium's Herbal Activity Hub. Kristine is the writer and illustrator of the online children's publication *Herbal Roots zine*, which has been published since 2009, and the creator of several online courses that teach children about botany, drawing, and herbs. Teaching others about plants and sharing her knowledge with children—our future—is her passion. Kristine lives on a homestead with her partner, their two youngest children, and a variety of cats, dogs, chickens, goats, and a bearded dragon.

CPSIA information can be obtained
at www.ICGtesting.com
Printed in the USA
JSHW010157260221
12006JS00001B/1

9 781647 398347